UP THE
DOVE!

By Mair Francis

DOVE Workshop
Roman Road
Banwen
Neath UK
SA10 9LW
www.doveworkshop.org

First published in 2008
© VIEW(DOVE) Ltd 2008
All Rights Reserved

ISBN 978-1-905762-72-9

An ICONAU production.

Cover photograph by Dean Cawsey
Designed and typeset by Lucy Llewellyn
Printed and bound by Dinefwr Press, Llandybïe, Wales
British Library Cataloguing in Publication Data

Contents

Glenys Kinnock receiving a bouquet of flowers from Sam Francis at the opening of the DOVE Workshop September 1987.

Foreword by Glenys Kinnock MEP

It is now over twenty years since I had the privilege of opening the DOVE Workshop in September 1987. I remember vividly the enthusiasm of those present for this completely unique initiative. Women had been inspirational during that bitter yet heroic struggle of 1984–85. They had been innovative in their campaigning to defend their communities now through DOVE and building a new future for themselves and their families.

I had known Mair Francis for over a decade before DOVE. I had also known, through the Labour Party activities and involvement in other progressive causes, the people of the Dulais Valley. It was no surprise to me that Mair and her friends were to be pioneers in the Dulais Valley in providing learning and training opportunities for women and the whole community following the destruction of the coal industry by the Tory Government of the 1980s and 1990s.

I have watched DOVE's progress over two decades and have been delighted by new developments, funded initially by an enlightened European equal opportunities strategy and now more recently by the Welsh Assembly Government.

DOVE is a shining beacon of progress for all the Valleys and for all former coalmining areas across Europe. Long may it continue to prosper.

From Humble Beginnings to a Centre of Excellence

A message from the founding chair of DOVE, Moira Lewis

On 5th June 1986 I became Chairman of DOVE during the same week that DOVE began its classes in Pantyffordd Hall. When the National Coal Board offered its opencast executive offices in Banwen to Onllwyn Community Council my immediate thoughts were to provide a home for DOVE. I became Chairman of Onllwyn Community Council in the November of 1986 and with the support of the Council DOVE was offered a home. By January 1987 the building was vacated by the Opencast Executive and leased to Onllwyn Community Council on the understanding that it should be used for educational and cultural activities and renamed Banwen Community Centre. I have a clear memory of Mair's delight when I took her to see the premises.

The Community Council gave DOVE use of the premises for one year (provisionally) free of charge provided it paid for heat and light. Mair wasted no time – she rallied her volunteers – they cleaned the premises and got to work with paint brushes and paint and really spruced the place up.

In February 1987 the classes commenced rapidly and a variety of activities developed with the support of partnerships with other agencies. Mair certainly had a 'vision' and met the challenge. She encouraged and motivated volunteers to take up training in a variety of subjects – leading to volunteers becoming tutors.

12th September 1987 was a very proud day when Glenys Kinnock officially opened DOVE Workshop and there was no doubt that Mair's 'vision' had become a reality, growing from strength to strength, with the present staff managed by Julie Bibby and Lesley Smith continuing to progress in all areas. Mair, Julie and Lesley are to be applauded for their hard work. I am extremely proud to have been associated with DOVE Workshop. May it long continue.

Moira Lewis

Neath Borough Council Member for Onllwyn 1976–96, Mayor of the Borough of Neath 1989–90 and Chairman of Onllwyn Community Council 1986–88

Acknowledgements

Inevitably much of what I have written in this short history comes from my own memories, documentation and discussions over the past two decades with friends in DOVE who helped establish and sustain the Workshop. I am eternally grateful to Moira Lewis, the founding chair of DOVE, who was a tremendous support, especially in the early formative years. I am also grateful to Julie Bibby, Lesley Smith and Susan Owen, who have sustained DOVE's progress for long periods and steered it to its present high level of development: they have given me invaluable insights into how the Centre has evolved since my departure in 1999. My thanks also go to Neath Borough Council and Neath Port Talbot County Borough Council, whose financial advice and support helped us through the years.

The early part of this history is based on my master's dissertation at Swansea University in 1995 entitled 'Women and the Aftermath of the 1984–85 Miners' Strike: A South Wales Analysis'. I wish to acknowledge the great support I received from Jane Elliot, Professor Angela John and Professor Teresa Rees in the completion of that research.

My life and work was sustained by the enthusiastic support of my family – Hywel, Hannah, Dafydd and most of all Sam who considered the crèche to be 'his crèche'. My mother, Hilda Hay Price, who now lives in the Dulais Valley, has been a real inspiration to me all my life and her feminism and socialism have undoubtedly shaped they way I have worked for DOVE.

I would like to thank the valiant women from 1984–85 Miners' Strike Support Group, particularly Kay Bowen, Marilyn James and Hefina Headon, for whom I have enormous admiration and respect and to whom I am eternally grateful since their sacrifices during that eventful year spurred us on to achieve something tangible for the future. Thanks also go to the members of the original Steering Group, especially Joy Howells who for many years chaired the DOVE committee with gentleness and purpose, and finally to the staff and students – past and present – for the way in which they have kept the faith with the ideals which founded the Workshop in the 1980s.

Mair Francis

UP THE
DOVE!

By Mair Francis

My Story, Our Story

This is a story, a personal journey, of women in the Dulais Valley, in the western anthracite coalfield of South Wales, following the bitter year-long Miners' Strike of 1984–85. It is a personal journey of hope that led to the creation of the women's co-operative, the DOVE Workshop in Banwen, at the northernmost point of the valley. Amongst the very first DOVE students were Lesley Smith and Julie Bibby. Since that time Lesley studied successfully for her degree at the centre and Julie qualified as a further education teacher.

They are now the managers of DOVE and both studying for the MA degree in Lifelong Learning at Swansea University. When Lesley and Julie asked me to write the history of DOVE, we were approaching twenty years of activities in the Banwen Community Centre. I was delighted and honoured to accept the challenge. They wanted me to pay tribute to the ideas and experiences of people I knew who had inspired me to set up a centre for women. I regarded the DOVE Workshop as 'my baby' since I nurtured it with tender loving care, grew annoyed with it when things went wrong, but was ultimately proud to see it growing up and maturing. I was recently made its President.

In 1972 I returned to South Wales from living and teaching in London with Hywel, my husband, and Hannah, our eighteen-month-old daughter, to live in Penrhos, Ystradgynlais, which still had the character of a traditional mining community although its last pit had closed in the 1960s. At first I was overwhelmed by the warmth and friendship from the community and at the same time concerned by the lack of provision for things that an urban community took for granted. I wanted to be active in the community and help to improve facilities; this was the beginning of my interest in community development. My work as a primary school teacher and evening class tutor gave me an added insight into the local valley communities.

After 1966, as a result of the Aberfan disaster, all coal tips in the South Wales valleys were being flattened and a new green environment was being formed. I became part of a campaign organised by 'green' villagers to fight for a cleaner community. In 1976, two years after the birth of our son, Dafydd, we had moved to Crynant (where there were still two collieries) in the Dulais Valley and in 1980 our third child, Sam, was born. Throughout this period, I was teaching in local schools, mainly Maesmarchog Primary School, which was located within the community where DOVE was eventually to be based.

In March 1984 the miners went on strike and as a family (my grandfathers were coalminers and tin plate workers) we immediately supported them in their struggle to defend their jobs and their communities. I had always had a dream to set up a co-operative and had attempted to establish a craft co-operative with Mair Bennett (who became a founder member of DOVE). In September 1984, six months into the strike, Phil Bowen, the Chairman of the Blaenant Lodge, told Hywel that his wife Kay was interested in setting up a co-operative. Kay was organising the feeding of over 1,000 families from the Neath, Dulais and Swansea Valleys Miners' Support Group (which Hywel chaired) and had many contacts with other women affected by the strike.

We held meetings in Kay's house and at first decided to set up a small business so that women could make money to supplement the family income – crucial during the strike. We had many offers of support and advice – the 'King of Hay', Richard Booth, bookseller and good friend of the miners, had ideas for us – but we wanted to develop our own ideas. We were not businesswomen but we knew that we had management skills that could be useful in setting up some kind of co-operative.

The strike ended in March 1985 and most of the women who were miners' wives were exhausted from the worry and despair brought on by a year of struggle. But a small group continued to meet. I took on the responsibility of fundraising and report writing. The story continues…

Women & Community Roots

This history will explore the past and current developments of the DOVE Workshop from the miners' strike 1984–1985, its development as a lifelong learning culture, the setting up of a social enterprise and essentially the story of how women from the Dulais Valley came together to make a difference.

This history will record the political, social and economic progress of the women and the communities of the Dulais Valley. The experiences of women in the miners' strike, the establishing of a women's co-operative in 1989 and the setting up of the collaborative strategy with other organisations – these were all part of the experiences of the founder members of DOVE.

The visibility of women in the strike and the change in traditional gender roles became the catalyst for change, and to meet those changes effectively it was necessary to equip the women with the appropriate skills for the workforce, to become multi-skilled and to widen the cultural, economic and social horizons by developing a holistic approach to education and training. This would include the implementation of equal opportunities measures, including crucially improved child care provision, family friendly work practices, home-based working opportunities, career breaks and opportunities for women to take up (or return to) education and training courses.

It was in this spirit of taking control in 1984–85 that women of all ages from a cross section of the community – teachers, factory workers, nurses, miners' wives, mothers and homemakers – came together in a struggle to protect and 'save their communities'. Their dynamism together with their organisational skills, their public speaking alongside male politicians, their demonstrations on marches and at picket lines were inspirational to all.

Following the strike, we established a crèche, transport support and part-time flexible delivery of education and training courses. This women-led initiative began to meet the needs of the whole community. For this the DOVE Workshop became recognised as an innovative community development and social enterprise initiative and acknowledged as an example of best practice by IRIS, the Women's Training Network of the European Union.

After two decades, this 'social partnership', this consensus of ideas established after one of the most bitter industrial disputes of the twentieth century – the miners' strike – now leads the way to economic regeneration in the Dulais Valley alongside another body which it subsequently helped to establish, the Dulais Valley Partnership.

Why DOVE?

DOVE Workshop was influenced by three radical social movements, the green movement, the peace movement and of course the women's movement. But it was also the trade union movement through the miners' strike which became the catalyst for the Workshop. We named our co-operative the Dulais Opportunities for Voluntary Enterprise (DOVE) Workshop so that its language would have a connection to the current political times. Enterprise was a 'snappy' expression and the voluntary sector was becoming increasingly proactive in many ways. We also needed to use this language in order to be successful in acquiring funding. The 'Workshop' was a radical term taken from the ideas of Joan Littlewood's Theatre Workshop (which had performed in the locality half a century before). Like the theatre, DOVE aimed to break the mould: Joan Littlewood did it to British drama and DOVE aimed to change women's place in a valley community, to create a space for women where they could find themselves and reach their full potential.

The dove symbol, taken from Picasso's distinctive image, was appropriate. The peace movement became a focus for social action and women's political activity. The women's peace marches started on 5th September 1981 when 'Women for Life on Earth', made up predominantly of Welsh women, arrived at Greenham Common, Berkshire, England. Marching from Cardiff, they challenged the decision to site 96 Cruise nuclear missiles at the Common. They 'feared for the future of all our children and for the future of the living world which is the basis of all life'.

The Dulais Valley had its own branch of the Campaign for Nuclear Disarmament (CND) and many of its members became passionate supporters, committee members and users of the

Hefina Headon speaking at a rally in Seven Sisters on 19th May 1984 during the miners' strike, with Phil Bowen, Chair of the Blaenant Lodge. (Photo by Norman Burns)

DOVE Workshop, namely Joy Howells, Norman Burns, Betty Miller and the late Doug Miller. The local CND banner, which I had made in the early 1980s, had Picasso's dove of peace as its centrepiece, exactly like the Seven Sisters miners' banner of the 1950s, with its powerful slogan, 'Y Byd Yn Un Mewn Heddwch' ('The World as One in Peace').

The green movement, like the peace movement, shaped the development of DOVE. At one time we were surrounded by opencast mining – a constant reminder of how the coal industry was capable of affecting our environment.

FUTURE PROGRAMME

MACHINE KNITTING FOR BEGINNERS
MACHINE KNITTING - ADVANCED
SPINNING & WEAVING

WOMEN'S HEALTH COURSE - Dr Mary Hoptroff, with U.C. Swansea.
WOMEN IN LITERATURE - Penny Windsor, with U.C. Swansea.
SCIENCE FOR WOMEN - Mary Miles, Carole Dicks, Sian Davies, with Neath Coll.
WORD PROCESSING - CERTIFICATE IN INFORMATION TECHNOLOGY, with Neath ITeC.
VIDEO PRODUCTION - with Neath College.
ELECTRICAL REPAIRS - with W.E.A.
ART - with, U.C. Swansea.
SETTING UP A SMALL BUSINESS OR COOPERATIVE - with W.G.C.O.D.A.

****

During the first year we have worked closely with outside agencies that are
now committed to strengthening links with the community.
Neath College, the Department of Adult Education at University College,
Swansea, and the Consortium for Adult Training (C.A.T.) are developing
policies which puts a greater emphasis on training related to local needs.
This significant change in the attitude of the role of Educators and
Trainers is all important since V.I.E.W. HAS BEEN PART OF THAT IMPORTANT
CHANGE.
The facilities at the D.O.V.E. Workshop enables the statutory organisations
to provide Community Based Training and Educational Skills.

31st March 1987

signed................

D.O.V.E. Workshop Manager.

VISITORS TO D.O.V.E. WORKSHOP

Jo Richardson	Member of Parliament
Marilyn and Paul Robeson Jnr.	New York, U.S.A.
John Kallabaka	Institute of Rural Development and Planning, Tanzania
Diana Conyers	Centre for Development Studies University College, Swansea
Chris Curling	B.B.C. Producer
Trevor Griffiths	Playwright, Yorkshire
David Brown	Poet, California, U.S.A.
Prof. Richard Shannon	Dean of Faculty of Arts, University College, Swansea
Peter Stead	History Dept, University College Swansea
Helen Cahill	Valleys Project, W.G.C.S.C.
Dilys Thomas	" "
Rona Howells	Neath Borough Council Training Agency
Richard Couto	University of Tennessee, U.S.A.
John Griffiths	Dean of Studies, Neath College
Dr. Brian Clarke	Adult Training Organiser, Neath Coll.
Graham Smith	Adult Education Advisor, L.E.A.
Roger Tovey	Consortium for Adult Training

DOVE programme listing visitors to DOVE in March 1987.

The DOVE building had been opencast offices. Ever vigilant of the changing landscape we aimed to raise awareness of its history, beauty and potential. This can be seen in the latest projects – the community garden and the landscaping around the Community Centre were projects developed through consensual partnerships.

The women's movement was probably the most influential of the social movements mentioned and is best understood by Bea Campbell and her view on masculinity. Bea was to speak at the centre in its early years. She wrote that

> The cult of masculinity in work and play and politics thrives only in exclusive free masonries of men with their secret codes which render women immigrants in their own communities.

The political activities experienced by the wives of miners during the miners' strike provided them with new skills to think beyond the immediate struggle and to forge a future for themselves, their families and their community. These women organised the distribution of food to 1,000 families, spoke on political platforms with miners' leaders and politicians about their personal experiences and began the networking with other women's groups throughout Britain.

After the miners' strike the two remaining collieries closed, Treforgan in September 1985 and Blaenant in May 1990.

Women in the valleys had little access to education or training, childcare or transport. There was a need to take control and make decisions for themselves. Soon after the ending of the miners' strike in May 1985, many prominent South Wales women spoke at a conference entitled 'Welsh Women Make History' in Onllwyn Miners' Welfare Hall. Looking back at that inspirational event, the speakers – future professors Angela John and Teresa Rees, now Bevan Foundation Director Victoria Winckler, film-maker Eileen Smith and celebrated writer Menna Gallie – all anticipated an exciting and innovative era for Dulais Valley women.

Later Professor Teresa Rees, Vice Chancellor Cardiff University, stated that

> DOVE was a pioneering venture in embedding equality into not just a curriculum but a whole way of delivering education and training to adults, especially women returning to learning after a break. In particular the courses were arranged to start where the women were at – in terms of childcare and other needs, confidence levels, skills and location. It was a landmark in learner-centred education and training. The international links made everyone realise how common some experiences were and what could be done to address them. DOVE went further than just being a provider however, it provided important documented lessons for mainstream providers. DOVE changed people's lives.

Welsh Women Make History conference at Onllwyn Welfare Hall 1985. From left to right: Dr Victoria Winckler, Dr Teresa Rees and Eileen Smith. (Photo by Hywel Francis)

The DOVE Workshop was seen as a prototype, the first of its kind in an industrial South Wales community that was besieged by the effects of Conservative Government policies of the 1980s which ran down the coal and steel industries.

Six months into the strike we were a strident, forceful group of women who were determined to use our personal experiences to initiate a unique development in our history. We were aware of our potential and realising it?

Towards the end of the strike I wrote in the *Valley Star* (the newspaper of the local support group) outlining our hopes and aspirations for better opportunities for women. Women were becoming increasingly confident and they wanted to move on from saving their communities towards a more tangible advancement that would offer them opportunities to improve their skills.

From now on some of their lives would take on a new direction. Kay Bowen, who had been given the responsibility by the Support Group as the overall food co-ordinator for three valleys, and many other women activists were concerned about the lack of job opportunities for women in an area of high unemployment. Women's employment was traditionally limited to low paid, low status and part time work. The Dulais valley was an area where women were predominantly economically inactive, with an inadequate and expensive transport service and a total lack of affordable childcare. Against this challenging background we decided to set up a workshop with these aims:

1. To provide facilities and an opportunity to teach women new skills, thus enabling them to seek quality employment.

The Miners' Struggle over the last 12 months is certainly part of the onslaught on our Class, and for lack of support, our men returned to work yesterday. We must pull together, learn certain lessons, and prepare for our next struggle. We must find the means of getting our message over to our class - they certainly need to be told what is facing them. They must be ready to resist all attacks from this vicious Tory Government, otherwise we'll all go under.

Our men back in work must never forget the support they have received in this country, and also all over the world. They must never be afraid again to support worthy causes wherever they may be. Capitalism must be opposed all over the world, and our Class must be ever ready to fight it thereby protecting ourselves. If we refuse to come together in solidarity, then our future will be forever bleak.

Our gratitude is extended to all you wonderful, understanding, dedicated people all over the country, and as we learnt from this conference, from all over the world as well. Of course, we must never forget the support we have received from our own people at home, especially the elderly people, they have contributed so generously and also played such a big part in raising money at our numerous functions. Our men and their families will never forget you - you have played such a tremendous role in sustaining them.

DULAIS OPPORTUNITY FOR VOLUNTARY ENTERPRIZE

A group of women have come together to set up a Women's Workshop to teach women both traditional and non traditional skills. We have applied for a Manpower Services Commission grant to renovate the Old Billiard Hall in Onllwyn. Unfortunately, this scheme has been held up, but we have been given the opportunity to renovate a small area of this building. We are hoping for electricians, carpenters, people with experience and inexperience in building renovation to give their time voluntarily to get this project off the ground. The project will commence on Monday March 18 at the Old Billiard Hall, Khartoum Terrace, Onllwyn, opposite Onllwyn Chapel at 9.00 am. If you are willing to help either turn up on the day, or if possible ring the following people to arrange your rota:

Mair Francis	Crynant	750677
Kay Bowen	Seven Sisters	700065
Marilyn James	Seven Sisters	701203
Hefina Headon	Seven Sisters	700703

INTERNATIONAL WOMEN'S DAY

Our Women's group have been invited to the Swansea Women's Centre for a social evening on Friday 8 March. There will be informal discussions and exchanges of ideas followed by a preview of the film being made by the Swansea Women's History Group about our women's activities. The evening will finis with a disco. All women are welcome. Anyone interested, please contact Margaret Donovan, Tel. 730388.

INTERNATIONAL WOMEN'S DAY RALLY - CHESTERFIELD - SATURDAY 9 MARCH

This is a very important rally, a chance fo women to show their involvement and commitment to the struggle against the destructio of their communities. Arthur Scargill will be the main speaker. There will be exhibitions, discussions, videos and street entertainment. A bus has been arranged by Swansea Support Group, and our women have been invited to share their coach free of charge. Anyone interested please contact Margaret Donovan, Tel. 730388.

THE SOUTH WALES WOMEN SUPPORT GROUPS

These are fighting to help re-instate the 42 miners in South Wales who have been sacked during the strike. There was a demonstration outside the NCB office in Llanis en last Monday, when a letter was given to Philip Weekes. The women wanted to arrange a discussion, but he is "too busy" until 29 March. The South Wales Women's Support Group lobbied the South Wales Area Conferen in Porthcawl on Friday 1st March telling th delegates not to forget these men. A lette was handed into the conference by Sian Jame of Caerbont, and it was read out to everyone there. It is our intention to keep thi issue in the forefront of everyone's mind.

ONLLWYN WELFARE HALL : 12 March

An Anniversary Concert will be held at the above Hall with guests; Colin Price and John Humphreys etc. Contact the Food Centre for tickets.

On 9th March at the above Hall Penrhyn North Wales Choir will perform, admission free.

Extract from The Valley Star, published by Neath, Dulais and Swansea Valley Miners Support Group. Printed by Glantawe Litho Printers. No. 31, 6th March 1985.

2. To provide childcare facilities for mothers of young children so that they could attend daytime classes.

3. To provide a flexible learning environment.

4. To provide transport to enable women to participate in such activities as were available.

The organising committee included Kay Bowen, Julie Rees, Marilyn James, Letty Jenkins, Christine Marshall, Mair Francis, Hefina Headon, Janet Thomas, Irene Craddock, Sonia Wheeler, Carys Davies, Mair Bennett and Susan Harris. The group met for meetings and classes in members' homes, until they were able to use an old, derelict billiard hall in Onllwyn. Subsequent to an unsuccessful bid for a grant from 'Opportunities for Volunteering' in November 1984, an application was made again in March 1985 and a grant of £600 was obtained in September 1985 to cover volunteer fees to establish a machine knitting co-operative and a community launderette. A new door and frame were purchased for the billiard hall costing £89.69. It was

from such small and humble beginnings that progress began to be made.

Success – Real Funding Won at Last!

The group successfully applied for an Urban Aid Grant from the Welsh Office and Neath Borough Council with the support of Councillor Moira Lewis. A total of £120,000 for three years was gained which enabled both DOVE and a group of women in Glynneath and their Glynneath Women's Employment Project (GWEP) to develop their projects. With no permanent banking facilities in the valley it was a challenge for DOVE to manage such a large grant.

From June 1986 I gave up my teaching job and I applied for, and was appointed as, the Manager of DOVE, and Caroline Summerfield was appointed as a part time nursery nurse, shared with the GWEP crèche. But with no building to work from progress was slow. The first 'official' meeting of DOVE was held on 5th June 1986 at Onllwyn Welfare Hall with new committee members including Jan Richardson, Judith James, Carol Stevens,

Humble beginnings – Onllwyn Billiard Hall 1984

Maria Bailey and Brenda Williams. A committee was elected at the meeting with Moira Lewis, the Borough Councillor for Onllwyn, as Chairperson, Brenda Williams as Secretary and Maria Bailey as Treasurer. At this first meeting the Onllwyn Community Council assisted us enormously by agreeing to allow the use of Pantyffordd Hall as temporary accommodation. It was at this meeting that the plans were discussed to establish the first class – a machine knitting class to commence on Wednesday 11th June 1986 at 9.30 am – and also agreed that the crèche should be made available to working mothers during the school holidays.

Pantyffordd Hall
June–December 1986

From June to December 1986 courses in machine knitting and spinning and weaving were running successfully at Pantyffordd Hall with future courses in computers to be held in another venue. A basic course in machine knitting started with five women and by December 1986 the class numbers had increased to nineteen. One of the course members, Liz Flaherty, who had some experience in spinning and weaving, was asked to develop a course in spinning, weaving and dyeing. This concept of developing local talent was an example of how DOVE would devise innovative learning opportunities: it really was curriculum development of a new kind.

In the first six months two significant questions were being raised. We questioned our rationale. How could we develop good practice and how could we give confidence to women to realise their full potential? There was a practical, pragmatic answer to this – we

Two managers and a nursery nurse were employed and the two groups came together and formed VIEW, the Valley Initiative for the Employment of Women. The synergy between the two groups strengthened the application and it enabled both groups to remain autonomous until their eventual amicable separation in 1994 when we were registered as VIEW (DOVE) Ltd as a company limited by guarantee and a registered charity within the voluntary sector.

needed to identify local talent and encourage new skills for all. Tutors and students alike needed to ensure that all provision was community-led and community-based, thus ensuring that course provision became genuinely organic, holistic and democratic.

Pantyffordd Hall was situated in a small hamlet between Onllwyn and Seven Sisters and was the venue for local meetings and performances of the local amateur dramatic society, and for that reason it was fully equipped with a stage and auditorium. However, it was inappropriate for DOVE's long-term needs. We drew up plans to renovate the old billiard hall at nearby Onllwyn. An application was made to the Manpower Services Commission (MSC) under the Community Programme for September 1987 to renovate the building and employ a driver, an administrative assistant and a caretaker/cleaner/cook.

At the same time, discussions took place which led to meetings with adult students from Fife, Scotland, at Swansea University. Trips were also organised to

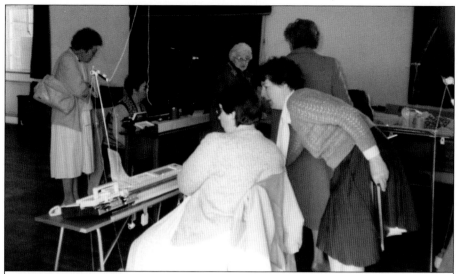

Joan Richardson MP (far left) visiting the machine knitting class in Pantyffordd Hall, 1986.

visit textile factories and textile printers, and attend weekend courses in machine knitting. Constant applications for further funding to local opencast mining companies were put together with the support of the DOVE committee. Invitations to speak on local radio were accepted. Purchasing both first-hand and second-hand equipment for the classes was arranged as well as making plans for the running and maintenance of a mini bus provided by the opencast Wimpey Mining Company.

The Workshop was a new phenomenon. We invited politicians to visit us. Jo Richardson, MP for Barking and Labour front-bench Spokeswoman on Women, who visited Pantyffordd Hall on Thursday 18th September 1986, was favourably impressed and she said that she hoped a future Labour Government would appoint a Minister for Women with Cabinet Status and that such an appointment would mean more help for groups such as DOVE. With that feed-back plans were put in place to ask Glenys Kinnock to open the billiard hall in September 1987 on completion of the renovations.

Whilst we were in our temporary accommodation it was impractical to organise a computing course, but the group wanted to develop these new skills and not 'go back' to 'gender specific' courses of shorthand and typing. I approached the Neath ITec Centre, financed by Neath Borough Council, who agreed to provide an 'Introduction to Word Processing' courses for eighteen women, on its premises at Milland, Neath, from July 1986 to January 1987.

Any future plans for the billiard hall had to be put on ice because by Monday 13th October 1986 it was confirmed that the roof tiles contained asbestos and their removal would have to be completed before any renovations took place. The cost of removal – £6,000 to £8,000 – was prohibitive. However, good news was on the horizon. On Monday 10th November 1986 Councillor Moira Lewis reported that although she had been informed that any renovations to the billiard hall had been ruled out, negotiations for the handover of the Banwen Offices of the National Coal Board Opencast Executive to the Onllwyn Community Council were progressing well and it was hoped that DOVE Workshop would be occupying a room there in the near future.

DOVE was at the stage of promoting its future programme and was asked to set up an exhibition stall at the Industry Year Exhibition at the Neath Civic Centre from 25th to 29th November 1986.

We Are on Our Way – Moving into Banwen at Last: January 1987!
I well remember the day when Moira Lewis showed me the Banwen Opencast

Executive Offices for the first time. It was situated off the no-through road terraced street of Roman Road on the edge of an opencast mining site. We were like two small children pressing our noses up against the window; we looked inside the main room, which was a drawing room with large slanting tables. I knew immediately that this would be the ideal place for the crèche.

These offices were vacated by the NCB during its 'rationalisation' programme in January 1987 and leased to Onllwyn Community Council on the understanding that the building should be used for educational and cultural purposes. Renamed the Banwen Community Centre, this substantial building with adequate space for a crèche, seminar and meeting rooms would also provide accommodation for the Department of Adult Continuing Education (DACE) of University College Swansea, which was looking for a base in the

DACE, UWS Art Tutor George Little with students Doris Hales and Vera Pinner.

Hefina Headon, Miners Support Group. Welcoming address at Summer Fete, 1987. (Photo by DOVE Workshop)

valleys to develop a more radical community-based education programme.

We moved in on 2nd January 1987 and DOVE was given the use of the building rent free for one year until 1st April 1987. With enormous enthusiasm, the group set about preparing the rooms in readiness to commence activities in February 1987. With the help of volunteers from both DOVE and GWEP we washed down walls, cleared away the hard hats, wellies and waterproof coats and proceeded to paint walls. Buckets, mops, paint, rollers and brushes were a permanent feature for a few weeks. The Urban Aid grant purchased carpets for the crèche and office and within the year we were employing tutors.

Linda Jones and Norma Thomas became the Machine Knitting tutors. Jen Francis was employed through West Wales Arts as the resident Hand Knitting tutor and taught women to knit with twenty or more colours. Liz Flaherty was the Spinning and Weaving tutor. Angie Dix, a designer knitter in Machine Knitting, brought another dimension to the courses. Karen Ronan was the IT tutor. Tim Exton and Trevor Thomas were the Video Production tutors and George Little from Swansea University was the Art Tutor.

We also purchased nursery equipment from West Glamorgan County Supplies, the same equipment that the infants and primary schools used. Fortunately there was a steel security room, an ideal place to store computers, and with more funding we were at last able to purchase our own computers and trolleys. Every day we wheeled out the computers on trolleys and every evening wheeled them back in again! Classes commenced in February and with the aid of the mini bus trainees/attendees were picked up for every class from the surrounding villages.

Developing the Learning Opportunities
Our funding did not stretch to covering tutor fees and we approached a local training consortium – DATEC, the Neath

13

District for Adult and Training and Education Committee which had been formed in February 1987. I was eventually elected as its secretary. It was made up of education and training providers from Neath College, the Workers' Education Association and voluntary sector providers, all sharing a common aim to develop education and training provision for all adults in their communities.

Our succesful application to the MSC in 1988 enabled us to employ three workers – Julie Bibby as a driver/clerk, Mair Harlock as an administrative assistant and Hefina Ferriman as an office support worker.

Replan was a project set up by the National Institute of Adult Continuing Education (NIACE) to encourage educational opportunities for adults and it produced a booklet in 1988 called 'Starting from Scratch', which included a case study of DOVE. Replan and DOVE applied jointly to the MSC to establish a WOW (Wider Opportunities for Women) course in computing in Banwen provided by the Port Talbot

Skills Centre. This collaborative approach enabled DOVE to develop a series of courses including a Women's Health course tutored by the Dulais Valley's local doctor, Dr Mary Hoptroff, and a local nurse, Diana Trott; Electrical Repair courses provided by the Workers' Educational Association (WEA); New Technology courses provided by MSC; taster courses with films and workshops on 'Setting up a Small Business or Co-operative', followed by a ten week course provided by Jenny Lynn of the West Glamorgan Common Ownership Development Agency (CODA); and Siân Davies, Mary Miles and Carole Dicks, science teachers from Neath College, providing a 'Science for Women' course to encourage women to attend the science laboratory at Neath College. This last course was for women who wanted to return to work as part-time laboratory assistants in schools and industry.

Future courses were to be Fly-tying; Sewing provided by Neath College; Welfare Rights; Italian Cities and the 'Romans in Banwen' provided by

Chilean dancers at DOVE Workshop Summer Fete 1987. DOVE Workshop surrounded by open cast mining. (Photo by DOVE Workshop)

Swansea University. Antur Teifi, an organisation that encouraged employment initiatives in rural Wales, approached DOVE to share a part of its stand at the National Eisteddfod at Fishguard during August 1986. We were breaking down barriers and creating a space for women and in this first year in Banwen we began to develop innovative partnerships and exciting new ideas.

Maggi Dawson, formerly Co-ordinator of Lifelong Learning, Neath Port Talbot County Borough Council, and now General Secretary/Chief Executive of the WEA, said of these times and subsequent developments:

The staff at DOVE – and in particular Lesley, Julie and Mair – have never ceased to amaze me with their continuing enthusiasm, energy, creativity and commitment. DOVE never stands still. It continued to live up to its name – providing ever-increasing opportunities for the people of the Dulais Valley and beyond, of whatever age. I have seen the building double in size, the organisation grow in influence and the staff grow in confidence and expertise.

DOVE is undoubtedly one of the best community-based organis-ations I know and is deservedly recognised as a model of best practice across the UK and Europe. I am certain that its legacy has already been felt by many and this history will ensure that its work continues to enthuse and inspire.

DOVE the Co-operative

During this early period CODA organised a business course with the staff in DOVE which gave us the confidence to register the DOVE Workshop as a workers' co-operative with Companies House. Subsequently it was registered as a community co-

> In 1989 the Workshop established a community co-operative to complement the educational arm of DOVE by improving the crèche facilities; offering a community-based desktop publishing service at affordable rates and providing technology training with a declared commitment to women-specific training.
> We set up DOVETALES Video Production, TURTLE DOVE Desktop Publishing, the OLIVE BRANCH Café and the DOVECOTE Nursery. All these were a precursor to the Social Enterprise initiatives so successful in Banwen today.

operative. This gave us a trading arm to provide additional benefits from the formal grant agencies.

It was generally agreed that to make an impact on developing community education it was crucial that DOVE developed a wide range of partnerships with other educational and training providers and community organis-ations. The first partners were the local elected representatives of the Onllwyn Community Council and Neath Borough Council. The next step was to forge links with the University at Swansea, Neath College and the WEA.

The Banwen Branch of the WEA was established in 1989. The role of DOVE, as a grass roots organisation, was to identify learners and set up informal learning opportunities that would provide a progression route into more formal education and training programmes.

At this time negotiations were taking place simultaneously with a number of organisations and individuals that would help DOVE to draw up ideas and develop into something tangible and sustainable. They included West Glamorgan County Council; Onllwyn Community Council; Neath Development Agency; Neath Borough Council's Planning Department; David Morris MEP; and Professor Doreen Massey, Director of the Greater London Enterprise Board and Professor of Geography at the Open University.

How the Funding Was Used

From the humble beginnings of receiving small grants, our journey was now taking another route. We had lofty ideals of setting up a co-operative to earn money and put something back into the community. But we soon became increasingly aware that we needed to learn more skills to achieve this aim. Education and training became the central focus of our work and by the end of the first year in Banwen we realised that the strengths within our community enterprise were the potential talents of the women themselves.

Many developments were now rapidly taking place. The Adult Education Department in Swansea University was expanding its provision in Banwen. A wide range of courses were successfully launched – a Welsh Intensive course; Art; Health for Men; Creative Writing with the author Alun Richards; a Writers Workshop course called Storyboard, teaching those interested in writing scripts/short stories; Soldiers in a Landscape: the Roman Army in South East Wales; Why Roman Road?, an archaeology class; History on Our Doorstep; Welsh for Beginners; Introduction to Computers; Further Investigation into Drawing and Painting.

The further development of women's

Aims and Objectives for April 1987 to March 1988

As with any organisation ideas change and flourish; DOVE is no exception to this. Within a few months of working from the Banwen Community Centre we needed to take stock and analyse carefully our new direction. And so we decided to broaden our aims and objectives but bear in mind our original ideas. These aims and objectives were:-

• To identify the educational and training needs of women.
• To establish and enhance the crèche facilities in Banwen
• To provide transport facilities for women in the valley and in the more isolated villages.
• To give advice, encourage and foster small businesses and co-operatives.
• To recruit volunteers and establish a Community Programme scheme with three part-time workers.
• To hold exhibitions, meetings etc.
• To raise funds and donations.

health courses run by Dr Hoptroff had built up its own network through the local hospital, surgeries and clinics. We began to develop day schools based at Pantyffordd Hall using the large auditorium for movement classes, self-defence classes for women with a health and well-being focus.

In 1988 Neath College and the WEA were providing courses in Spanish, French, yoga, and sewing and day schools such as 'From Fleece to Fabric' which showed a film of women from the Shetland Isles called 'Our Work Is Our Own' alongside workshops in machine knitting, spinning, weaving and hand knitting. Other day schools were 'Women and Video', a day of film and video about women in work, their feelings, opinions and aspirations. 'Bend It, Shape It; Anyway You Want It!' was a workshop on keep-fit, circle dancing and self-defence for women. A short film was shown about a woman weight lifter and her

training programme. 'Your Health, Your Choice' was a day of practical workshops to teach men and women to take responsibility for their own health, and 'Environment' was a day school on the environment and its effect on our lives.

Other activities were workshops at weekends for women returners provided by the Wider Opportunities for Women programme, sharing the crèche provision with the local playgroup, recruiting staff in the crèche, providing lunches and snacks for children and those attending classes. The University was providing courses in introductory and advanced Welsh; Art; a writers' workshop; English; History; 'Healthy Living for Men'; Computer Literacy; 'Science for Women'; and Geology. DOVE was now being asked to participate in conferences organised by the Cardiff and Swansea Women's Road-shows.

In the spring of 1987 the video

Day school at Pantyfford Hall: 'Bend It, Shape It, Anyway You Want It', May 1988. (Photo by DOVE Workshop)

production course established the co-operative DOVETALES Production co-ordinated by Gillian Davies and Sonia Wheeler. They made three films, on Henrhyd waterfalls, on the DOVE Workshop and its activities and one about changing village life in Banwen. All this was done with the help of Chapter Arts Video Workshop from Cardiff. Also involved were Red Flannel Films, a women's workshop operating from Pontypridd. 'MAM' was the first major film production by Red Flannel Films, which was an organisation similar to DOVE that also grew out of work undertaken during the miners' strike. With this support the video production project established a network of media related initiatives such as the Valley Pictures network and a Video Camera Club that successfully showed screenings of independent films.

Our big day was on 12th September 1987 when Glenys Kinnock officially opened the DOVE Workshop and she paid tribute to DOVE and its significant contribution to the lives of the people in the community – particularly to the women's lives. Glenys praised the enterprise and determination of DOVE and its recognition of the importance of providing opportunities and real choices for women, and expressed the hope that she would be invited back within the year. Over a hundred people attended the event including the Mayor and Mayoress of Neath, Councillor Iris Hobbs and Mr Tom Hobbs, Mr George Griffiths, the Chief Executive of Neath Borough Council, Mr David Morris MEP, Mr Reg Criddle from British Coal, Mr Elton Morgan of Wimpey Mining and Dr Hywel Francis of Swansea University, along with many tutors and students. An exhibition of art and craft work was open to the public during the week.

We were proud of our achievements in such a short time. Facing the challenge of establishing a centre in an area of industrial change was at times both frustrating and exciting. Our partnership with Swansea University's Department of Adult Continuing Education, Neath College and the WEA enabled DOVE to improve the quality and choices of courses for all adults. Although we were keeping to our commitment to women-specific training we were also developing a provision for all adults who wanted to enrol on Access to Higher Education courses. Partnership links were developing further and we were now working with NIACE (the National Institute for Adult and Continuing Education) and UDACE (the Unit for the Development of Adult and

Official opening of the DOVE Workshop. Reg Criddle of British Coal, Cllr Moira Lewis, Elton Morgan of Wimpey Mining, Glenys Kinnock, Mair Francis. (Photo by Evening Post)

Continuing Education), both national bodies that wanted to promote our work in community education provision.

Grass roots voluntary organisations like DOVE were having a significant impact on adult education provision which made the statutory sectors in local authorities and further and higher education sit up. One such organisation, the Valleys' Initiative for Adult Education (VIAE), was set up as a response to these changes and as a sign of DOVE's growing significance. VIAE held its first meeting at the Centre. VIAE was a 'network of statutory and voluntary organisations concerned with the role of Adult Education in the survival and development of valley communities'. It produced a publication called 'Next Step for the Valleys: regenerating Valley communities through Adult Education', in which the work of DOVE was featured prominently.

The membership of VIAE included Local Educational Authorities, universities in South Wales, the Open University and community-based organisations like DOVE and Amman Valley Enterprise (AVE) which was established in 1988. Maggi Dawson, a former Director of AVE, said of DOVE that it 'led the way

and became the model for the young AVE and that DOVE's staff and volunteers became AVE's mentors and our friends'. Other member organisations based in the valley communities which were inspired by DOVE included the Rhondda BELL Centre, now called Blaenllechau Community Regeneration, and the Bryncynon Community Revival Strategy at Mountain Ash in the Cynon Valley.

Recognising Quality and Progress

On 2nd December 1988 VIAE held a conference at Onllwyn Welfare Hall. It

Move to reel in the Valley audiences

Returning to magic of the big screen

A NEW initiative to bring back the magic of the cinema to South Wales valley areas has been launched.

Local groups in 10 centres in the area have been formed to manage and plan film shows this autumn and winter.

The scheme, co-ordinated by Valley Pictures, got under way at Onllwyn in the Dulais Valley on Monday night.

From now until the end of March people in valley and areas not near a public cinema will have the chance to see some of the top British, American and European films at a cheap rate.

Nostalgia

At Onllwyn Miners' Welfare Hall on Monday night, for example, My Left Foot with Oscar-winning actor Daniel Day-Lewis went on show.

To officially launch the season veteran Welsh actress Rachel Thomas opened the Onllwyn show.

By Jonathan Isaacs

A near capacity audience was there for opening night, auguring well for the future of the project which may be extended beyond next March if it is a success.

Valley Pictures says the aim is to bring back the nostalgia of going to the cinema.

"There's just nothing to match seeing films on a big screen with an appreciative audience," said a spokesperson.

But many people have got out of the habit of going to the pictures: in 1965 there were more than 200 cinemas between Swansea and Newport but now this number has dropped to less than 20.

Location

"We'll be showing a carefully selected programme of 12 films in 10 places across South Wales until the end of March and if the first season is as successful as we hope

further seasons will follow with films chosen by the audiences themselves," said the spokesperson.

Films will move from one location to another over two weeks and local centres include the Swansea College Art Centre; Onllwyn Miners' Welfare Hall; Glamorgan House in Cymmer Afan in the Afan Valley; and at the Brecon Arms in Ystradgynlais in the Swansea Valley.

There is a 50p fee to join Valley Pictures and films include Cinema Paradiso and Babbette's Feast-winners of the 1989 and 1990 Oscars for best foreign film; Trop Belle Toi, the great French success with no fewer than five French stars; Shirley Valentine with Pauline Collins; and the best film Oscar winner of 1990, Driving Miss Daisy.

"We aim to involve our members, the audience, in running and planning the shows, a truly democratic cinema," said the Valley Pictures spokesperson.

VETERAN Welsh actress, Rachel Thomas, is shown the night's programme by co-ordinator Mair Francis as she opens Valley Pictures' first film in Onllwyn. Also pictured are projectionist, Gerwyn Howell and Pearl Berry of Red Flannel Films.

"With practically any film ever made anywhere available to us to show, future seasons can be chosen by

the people who want to see them.

"Ours is a bold experiment aiming to bring

back a marvellous entertainment and social experience that thousands miss," said the spokesperson.

Valley Pictures' first film in Onllwyn with veteran Welsh actress Rachel Thomas, projectionist Gerwyn Howells, Mair Francis and Pearl Berry of Red Flannel Films, 1990. (Article & photo from Evening Post) was at this conference that I presented a 'Database' project that was a statistical study of those attending the Workshop. This work strengthened our funding applications so that the Neath Borough Council agreed to give us a further two years of funding. It included the number of attendances from June 1986 to March 1987, from April 1987 to August 1988 and from September 1988 to December 1988, with attendance increasing from under thirty to over one hundred and twenty. DOVE covered a wide catchment area with 57% coming from the Dulais Valley, 5% from the Neath Valley, 27% from the Swansea Valley, 2% from the town of Neath, 5% from Swansea, 4% from other towns. Overwhelmingly, travel to DOVE was by using the minibus, sharing lifts and walking. Most of the users of DOVE were over twenty-five years old representing 60%. Seven percent were under twenty-five and 33% represented the over fifties. (The over fifties group were made up mostly of the older women attending the Machine Knitting City and Guilds Course.) Twenty-two percent of those using the centre also used the crèche representing twelve children.

DOVE education and training programmes were aimed specifically at women who were under-represented in the workforce. But it became increasingly important that as a community-based organisation we should also provide courses to meet the needs of all from the community. Nevertheless we have never forgotten our central mission, supported by the European Social Fund (ESF) with its objectives to promote equal opportunities and new means of combating all forms of discrimination and inequalities in the labour market, both for those in work and for those seeking work.

After completing the first year's project, the next step was to seek employment outside the confines of the 'comfort zone', the DOVE Workshop. The staff on the MSC successfully moved on. Hefina Ferriman was employed at Neath College's Library, Mari Hurlock was employed at the Education Department's Library at Swansea University and Julie Bibby remained at DOVE and was employed as an Outreach worker for the WEA. As part of Julie's new role, she organised a taster programme for women that included make-up demonstrations, introduction to computers, cookery and the promotion of women's films. Lesley Smith attended the taster week and subsequently offered to work as a volunteer. With my encouragement she joined a government training scheme, with work experience in DOVE.

The showing of films, especially those made by women, was becoming very popular and gave the opportunity for those interested in film production and those who enjoyed independent feature films to attend viewings in the locality. Film Day Schools were organised and a Film Club showed films during the afternoon and evening over a period of six weeks, all with the help of West Glamorgan Video and Film Workshop and Swansea Women's History Group. This was all funded by West Wales Arts.

The adult learners' body NIACE was proactive in developing effective locally based education guidance networks for all adults in Wales. I attended one of the seminars and I was asked to be a member of the TUC Steering Committee for Centres for the Unemployed.

Gillian Davies and Sonia Wheeler filming during the 'From Script to Screen' course. (Photo by DOVE Workshop)

Video production course: 'From Script to Screen', 1989. (Photo by DOVE Workshop)

Action shots outside DOVE Workshop with Onllwyn Washery screens in the background. (Photo by DOVE Workshop)

Within a few short years, DOVE had become a well established social centre for women and men in the Dulais Valley. I realised this the moment I overheard groups of women talking, with eager anticipation, about going 'Up the DOVE'! This meant that it had become part of the fabric of our valley's community, in a very short time.

DOVE Workshop
Banwen Community Centre
Roman Road, Banwen

a new course

DIS-EASE & WHOLENESS
Women and Health
in Today's Society

starting on
Monday 6th February 1995

1.00 p.m. to 3.00 pm
for 20 weeks

This course explores the deeper potential for health and healing which lies within each woman. This course will address both the orthodox and complimentary approaches to wholeness on physical, psychological and spiritual levels.

The course fees are: £36/£18/£10

If you are interested and would like more information
Please ring: 0639 700024

d.o.v.e. workshop

DOVE Workshop
Women, Technology
& Enterprise in the Workforce

Course includes modules on:
Information Technology
Desk Top Publishing
Telematics
Women into Management
Funded through the NOW programme

Branwen Community Centre, Roman Road,
Branwen, Neath, SA10 9LW.
Tel: 0639 700024   Fax: 0639 701528

Canolfan Cymuned y Banwen, Heol Rhufeinig,
y Banwen, Castell Nedd SA10 9LW.

From fleece to fabric
with a difference.

DEPARTMENT OF ADULT EDUCATION
UNIVERSITY COLLEGE OF SWANSEA
In association with
The Valley Initiative for Employment of Women
and

Neath
IT EC
Information Technology
Centre
SPONSORED BY
NEATH BOROUGH COUNCIL

Posters advertising course provision.

Wider European Horizons

Developing Technology Provision – Women In Technology

The Women In Technology courses (affectionately called WIT) developed organically from the introductory courses to computers. In the aftermath of the miners' strike we prioritised technology training for women to enable them to transform their lives. To achieve this we looked for funding support outside Wales. The European Social Fund's four pillars within Objective Three – improving employability, development of entrepreneurship, encouraging adaptability and promoting equal opportunities – were the support structures that we knew would help develop the aims and objectives of the DOVE Workshop. It was the European Commission's plan to implement this strategic framework that supported measures to combat and prevent unemployment, develop human resources and promote social integration and equality in the labour market. This became our focus and still is.

By 1992 Susan Owen, who had trained on the computer courses, took further training, as had Julie Bibby previously, to become a tutor for the Advanced Professional Training Unit at DACE. This Unit was responsible for accessing European funding to support under-represented women in computer training. It was in this very early period

Joy Howells, Chairperson of DOVE Workshop, and Nuzat Javid, student on the 'Women in Technology' course. (Photo by DOVE Workshop)

that DOVE was looking at ways to 'on-line' the community, to link it to the emerging internet. We were a decade ahead of our time.

DOVE was now at the stage of developing the skills of the voluntary and paid staff alongside those of the trainees. Michelle Howells was appointed Nursery Nurse following Caroline Summerfield's departure. There were now over twenty-four children attending the crèche. These numbers enabled the Nursery Nurse, previously shared with Glynneath, to work almost on a full-time basis in the DOVE crèche. Mary Bryce began work as volunteer nursery assistant and Lisa Butler and Melanie Regan who were studying for their BTEC National Diploma at Neath College were placed with DOVE for their work experience.

Obtaining European funding to support our new ideas spurred the staff on to bigger and more exciting projects. Such funding allowed us to learn from other European women's organisations and this proved to be very fruitful.

Access to Higher Education

As students progressed, they grew in confidence, aspiration and ambition. Providing Access to Higher Education courses was the natural progression from the community-based learning courses at Banwen. The first Access to Higher Education modules were provided by DACE in 1989. Neath College provided Access to Health and Social Care which was a part-time course with the first year being delivered in Banwen and subsequent years at Neath College. Students from these courses progressed to the BA Humanities or BA in Nursing and Diploma in Social Work courses.

Valleys Women's Roadshow

We were very conscious of linking with other women's initiatives. The Valleys Women's Roadshow provided this for us: it was a three-year project that ran from March 1993 to March 1996. It was an organisation that aimed to: raise awareness of training and education opportunities for women; highlight the needs and barriers facing women; support and encourage women in gaining access to learning opportunities and work in partnership to widen opportunities for women. It was set up as a response to the many women's groups that were promoting women's potential and began to co-ordinate women's groups throughout the South Wales valleys into a strong effective network.

It achieved this by researching existing provision. It identified unmet needs, targeted under-resourced areas, organised events focusing on women, provided an extensive information service and set up local networking groups.

By looking to the future it aimed to increase the take-up of education, training and employment opportunities by women, improved the opportunity for women to be well informed, provided feedback of research to providers and policy makers and improved provision to meet the needs of women. Amongst those involved was Lynda Lumb, who was to become Welsh Woman of the Year in 1995.

New Credits through the Open College Network

From 1990 to 1995 I was seconded on a part-time basis to become the Development Officer for the South West Wales Open College and Access Consortium (SWWOCAC) which would prove invaluable to DOVE's development of credit-based learning. DOVE developed learning strategies to enable people to participate and succeed. This type of accreditation and qualification helped to secure DOVE's provision and made sure it was relevant to both the learners at DOVE and local employers. It offered robust standards, achievable goals and progression opportunities for all. The mission statement of the Open College Network

aimed to widen participation and access to high quality and flexible education, training and learning, to promote social inclusion and to ensure that learner achievement is recognised, valued and understood through a national framework of accreditation.

By 1993 community-based accredited progression routes at DOVE led to the launch of Swansea University's Community University of the Valleys at the Banwen Centre.

By April 1995 we put together our second evaluation project. This synergised the activities at DOVE with a

OCN Framework

The Open College Network recognises learning activities and award credits for learners' achievements.

Level One
A foundation level for skills necessary in everyday life.
Level Two
Introduces craft and artistic skills, learning to learn skills, language and maths, information technology and group skills.
Level Three
Acquisition of basic concepts to achieve functional competence in language, maths, creative and interpretative arts and information technology.
Level Four
This level prepares for entry to higher education or other professional training.

strategy to regenerate the local economy. This centred on the education and training provision provided by DOVE, WEA, DACE and Neath College that included courses such as women's health, languages, information technology, the Access to Higher Education and the University's Community University of

Banwen Community Centre before renovations, 1991. (Photo by DOVE Workshop)

the Valleys part-time degree programme. The report quantified and evaluated the outcomes of the first two years. It was a three-year programme that monitored and evaluated the skills-based needs of the local labour market with constant reference to the changing employment needs of the coalfield communities. The project liaised with local employers, training and education providers, community groups, local community services and community development strategy groups.

The evaluation project's research identified that the Banwen Community Centre was based in one of the most deprived wards in the South Wales valleys and was also the twenty-fourth

> There were twenty-nine programmes provided by DOVE, DACE, Neath College and the WEA..
> Forty-five percent successfully gained employment although the time lapse between training and work varied from immediate to three years.

most deprived of 908 wards in Wales. Thirty-two percent of under 25s (male and female) in the NPTCBC area were unemployed compared with 36.5% in Wales and 34% in the UK. Only 60% of women aged 16–59 and 77% of men aged 16–64 were economically active; 8.7% of women aged 16–59 and 13% of men aged 16–64 were permanently sick. This information indicated that the Dulais Valley had economic and locational problems as well as a background of under-performance and decline. This represented the scale of the challenge for the DOVE Workshop. From the very beginning Neath Borough Council and, subsequent to local government changes in 1996, Neath Port Talbot County Borough Council was the means by which we accessed funding, support and advice.

The evaluation project was an important exercise for us to be able to evaluate and monitor our work in order to strengthen our applications for further funding and progress our ideas. Funded through the Strategic Development Scheme from the Neath Borough Council, it enabled us to employ staff who could collate information related to student profiling, skills needs and education and training progression routes.

The project held information on personal details, peer group, gender, ethnic group, course details, qualifications and employment. In the period 1996/97, 304 participants were registered on the database. It proved that DOVE was steadily increasing its number of participants and those participants were progressing to work or further training.

In 1995/96 there were 201 participating and within one year there had been an increase of 50%. Of these numbers 82% were women and 18% were men, predominately from the 25–50 years age group, and 46% came from the immediate catchment area: Seven Sisters (34%), Dyffryn Cellwen (21%), Crynant (18%), Coelbren (13%), Banwen (9%), Onllwyn (3%) and Pantyffordd (2%). Thirty-three children used the crèche, ninety-one men and women using the centre were employed and 16% had no qualifications. Between 81 and 84% had vocational qualifications and a small percentage had A levels and degrees.

The database information was able to demonstrate the increased activity at DOVE from 1995 to 1998 and that the anticipated key outcomes of progression to work, further education and personal development had been successfully achieved.

Our plans to set up a community enterprise provided new training programmes for participants to realise their full potential. Every course enabled adults to learn skills to assist their learning and to gain knowledge of the labour market. Further developments were to create and sustain employment in support of the charitable aims.

Working Together for Regeneration

Voluntary and community organisations played a vital part in the regeneration of former mining communities. We also witnessed in this period the growing

Moving on from DOVE

From the outset the four following identifiable exit (from courses) routes were related to tangible outcomes, i.e. every participant achieved something and indicated a high level of achievement.

They were:

1. Progression to further education or training.
2. Progression to higher education provision.
3. Evaluation of personal development.
4. Effective competition in the labour market.

The DOVE Workshop's role had matured and we were becoming more sophisticated in our approach to our work. DOVE's role had always been and continued to be that of an agent for change for both individuals and whole communities. This approach has raised the aspirations of adults to seek skills that would help to regenerate the economic, social and cultural base of their community.

importance of strengthening the relationship between local government and the voluntary and community sector.

Dulais Valley Partnership Ltd was established in 1996, as a result of the strong partnerships and networks in existence. A development trust with holistic aims to regenerate our valley, it brought together key partners such as Neath Port Talbot County Borough Council, Neath College, Swansea University, West Wales Training and Enterprise Council, DOVE Workshop, British Telecom and the Community Development Foundation, along with local residents and small and medium sized enterprises (SMEs) to give the projects and process a genuine sense of community ownership. With its Strategy for Regeneration in 1996, the Dulais Valley Partnership nurtured developments in tourism and the environment, arts and culture, youth development and transport.

Looking to Europe and Women's Training

Funding issues have always been a bugbear throughout most projects. DOVE needed to take full advantage of European funds to develop our women-specific provision and develop ourselves as trainers and project managers. We were learning from other women's groups in Wales, particularly the South Glamorgan Women's Workshop, Women in Technology courses organised by Beverley Pold at Lampeter University and the research being carried out by Professor Teresa Rees. All this was helping us to identify the barriers to women's participation in education, training and employment.

As a result we knew that we had to promote non-traditional courses such as

computer technology for women, to run alongside the traditional machine knitting and sewing classes. The interest in the non-traditional courses was remarkable. Women were particularly interested in the new technology courses. Learning this skill would improve their chances of competing effectively in the labour market alongside men. This became a burning issue since women in mining communities have historically worked in low paid, low status and part-time work in gender-segregated areas such as the services sector and on the assembly lines in local factories. DOVE gave them new hope. We were able to purchase computer equipment with the help of various funding sources.

The decline of the mining industry in the valley was paralled by the growth of the service sector. According to Teresa Rees this led to a decrease in skilled full-time male employment and a growth in semi-skilled and unskilled female work in the service sector. This was reflected in our catchment area in that the female employment patterns represented a fluctuation

In her paper 'Feminising the Mainstream', Professor Rees states that in 1987, the European Commission drew attention to the need for equal treatment by adopting a Recommendation on Vocational Training for Women. This called upon member states to ensure that women have equal access to all types and levels of vocational training, particularly those professions likely to expand in the future, and those in which women have been historically under-represented.

between full- and part-time work. The only employment that some young girls aspired to was working in the local factories, such as the Dewhirst clothing factory and the instrument factory in Ystradgynlais affectionately called 'the Tick Tock' (both now long disappeared, production having moved to North Africa and Eastern Europe respectively).

This changing work pattern re-inforced not only a wages gap but also a skills gap. We wanted to challenge this and offer women the chance to attend courses in the day so that they were free to work. Professor Rees paid tribute to DOVE for putting into practice new progressive strategies for women and we were happy to host many conferences and day schools where Professor Rees explained the issues within a European context. She was often fond of promoting equal opportunities strategies which did not 'tinker' or even 'tailor' but 'transformed'. Now Pro-Vice Chancellor at Cardiff University, Teresa Rees was at this time in the 1990s a Reader at the School for Advanced Urban Studies, University of Bristol, and a consultant to the European Commission on women and training.

Overcoming Barriers

We were always conscious of our hopes and vision for the community. We were determined to use our personal exper-iences to initiate a unique development in our lives. We recognised our potential and wished to realise it every day. From the beginning our courses were under-pinned by support mechanisms to over-come barriers and to facilitate easy access to education and training courses. It was easy for us to recognise the barriers: we

Chwarae Teg

Chwarae Teg, established in 1992, supported, developed and expanded the role of women in the Welsh economy. It has promoted women's economic development across Wales and challenged stereotypes in employment and education.

As well as carrying out research across a range of issues affecting women in Wales, Chwarae Teg has been working with European partners to close the gender pay gap. Currently responsible for rolling out the Welsh Assembly Government's Work Life Balance programme across Wales, Chwarae Teg champions the flexible working ethos and supports women in enterprise and business.

lived and breathed them. These barriers were specific to women. Gender divisions within a mining community had been central to the fabric of every mining village and were ingrained and extremely slow and difficult to change. Jane Aaron, a senior lecturer in English at the University College of Aberystwyth, and Teresa Rees emphasised in their introduction to the book *Our Sisters' Land* the importance of the support women give to each other as they negotiate change:

> And that such supportive sisterliness has, of course, always been a key factor in feminist social change; nor is it surprising that a co-operative spirit should be particularly evident when the influence of feminist ideas is felt in close-knit communities, such as those in Wales.

Julie Bibby, Lesley Smith and Joy Howells learning about new technology, 1992.

To encourage women to make that very **BIG** step we needed to remind our-selves that we had an advantage over the larger institutions merely because we were able to deliver for local people within their local community. We would guarantee at a local level that childcare provision and transport support were free, women tutors were employed and became role models and course hours were designed around school hours and terms. Therefore flexibility was built into the courses. We were building on the traditions of the classes provided by the WEA, the local authorities and the National Council for Labour Colleges but broadening it, 'thinking outside the box' and developing and locating it within in an equal opportunities context.

Our partnership with other providers was working well: they provided the teaching expertise and we provided the 'students', the venue, the crèche and the transport. But we needed to develop our ideas more broadly and by looking to Europe we could see many benefits. Alongside the computer courses in DOVE now provided by Swansea University in partnership with Neath ITec and Neath Borough Council, we wanted to go further and broaden the choices. In 1988 we applied for a grant from the Equal Opportunities Commission to set up a project to purchase video production equipment to make a film called *Changing Opportunities for Women in the Dulais Valley, Past, Present and Future*.

This project was to be managed by the DOVETALES Video Production Unit that had grown out of the video production course. Unfortunately we were unlucky and failed to get the grant. However, that did not deter us and in 1989 we successfully applied for a grant to the European Social Fund's Objective Two programme to set up a video production training course for one year. With the help of Dr Victoria Winckler we got to grips with the procedure of applying for European funds. This was to be the watershed because we could expand our provision with financial support but also be taken more seriously by other funders.

IRIS – the Women's European Training Network

In 1991 DOVE became a member organisation of the Women's European Training Network IRIS, whose mission statement aimed:

> To increase the general levels of skills and knowledge, community co-operation and integration and at improving the status of women as a group which suffers systematic discrimination and unequal treatment in the labour market.

In April 1992 IRIS organised a visit to the Istituto Formazione Orientamento Lavoro Donne (IFOLD), a training organisation in Sardinia, Italy. I was selected to represent the United Kingdom on this European delegation involved in training women from six European countries. Heather Pudner from the Guidance Unit at DACE in Swansea University accompanied me since the projects under examination in Sardinia also delivered extensive guidance and

Benefiting from Europe was an interesting concept. Learners from DOVE had the benefit of travel, giving them access to the pavement café culture which was liberating. But the real benefits we were seeking would advance the social, economic and political opportunities for women. There were three beneficial areas that had a significant influence on the development and progress of the DOVE Workshop. They were:

1. Involvement in gaining funding from the European Social Fund to focus on women-specific training.
2. IRIS and the transnational exchange visits.
3. Guidance and counselling.

counselling programmes. There were similarities between the aims and objectives of DOVE and IFOLD since both practised a holistic approach to training with particular reference to the embedding of guidance and counselling within all training courses.

The partnership link with VIA (Vervolmakingscentrum voor Industrieeltechnische Applicaties) from the former coalmining area of Hasselt in Belgium came about as a result of a transnational training exchange in September 1992. Through the IRIS Network VIA chose DOVE Workshop as a suitable partner since geographically, socially and educationally there existed potential commonalities. Links were subsequently strengthened not only with VIA but with IFOLD and the Fundacion Dolores Ibarruri (FDI) from Spain at the IRIS Fair/Forum in Brussels 5–7

October 1992. FDI was from the Asturias coalfield in Spain and named after the hero of the Spanish Civil War. DOVE was contacted by Dolores Ibarurri's daughter to set up a partnership but unfortunately the partnership never materialised.

The IRIS Network gave the staff at DOVE opportunities to meet other women's organisations in Europe and on 6th October 1992 Julie Bibby, Lesley Smith and I travelled to Brussels to the Anspach Expo Centre to attend the IRIS Network Trade Fair and Conference. The WDA paid the transport and cost of the exhibition stand. British Coal Opencast

> **IFOLD** was set up in 1986 by a group of experienced teachers to establish training provision specifically for women. In Sardinia there had been an increase in work segregation and women were relegated to lower areas of work in the service industries. IFOLD responded to this situation by organising courses for the integration of women into professions where they were under-represented, thus breaking the mould and offering a chance of employment where no gender mould existed.
>
> The courses were information technology; business and co-operative skills; 'Telematics' taught skills to establish a 'help line' to older people without family or economic support. Called SOS, it used the caring skills of women as the strengths of the course; it also provided training in equal opportunities and positive action and women's history and guidance.

paid for the accommodation. It was at this conference that DOVE met again with IFOLD and with VIA to put together the plans to develop a European project, entitled 'Women in the Workforce', which concluded with a seminar in DOVE in November 1993. DOVE also met women from the Dunfermline Women's Training Centre in Fife and they were invited to the Women in the Workforce seminar in October 1993.

EMPLOYMENT NOW Initiative (New Opportunities for Women)

This was another funding-stream for DOVE. It was part of a European Union Employment Initiative and funded by the European Commission under the European Social Fund (ESF). It recognised that full participation of women in economic life was a necessity both with regard to equal treatment and for economic growth. It aimed to reduce unemployment, to increase opportunities in the labour market for women and to improve the position of those already in the workforce through the promotion of equal opportunity strategies. A key priority of EMPLOYMENT NOW was to integrate the results of innovative measures undertaken and developed by NOW projects into mainstream training and labour market systems. The women who would benefit from a NOW training course were those who were unemployed or threatened by unemployment, women returning to work, women wanting to establish their own enterprises, those seeking career advancement, women who were entering male-dominated areas, lone parents, women with low or no status qualifications, those on low pay, in low status employment or facing structural inequalities in mainstream education training and employment. Those directly involved were women participants, women's groups, social partners, trainers, human resource managers, development agents, equal opportunities advisors, staff in training/ local development and information centres and worker representatives responsible for negotiation on training issues.

Women continued to encounter specific obstacles to vocational employment and enterprise opportunities. There were and still are a whole range of inequalities experienced by women in the labour market as evidenced by their under-representation in managerial and decision-making positions and their over-representation in jobs which are marginal, insecure or badly paid. Within public and private organisations, procedures and practices are not always gender inclusive in their operations. Access to training, education and employment is often denied to women, particularly those living in disadvantaged or marginalised circumstances.

New Opportunities for Women Project 1993

DOVE obtained a grant from EMPLOYMENT NOW in 1993 for an information technology and personal development programme for women, for a transnational seminar to study employment for women in coalfield areas, for opportunities to exchange relevant course documents, to meet through exchange visits, to communicate through telecommunications and to document our shared similarities and differences. We called this project 'Women in the Workforce – Alternative Choices for Women in Coalfield Areas'. The steering group was supported by Lynette Grey, Economic

Women in the Workforce: European partners from VIA, Belgium, and IFOLD, Italy, with David Morris MEP at the New Opportunities for Women project conference, October 1993.

Development Officer from Neath Port Talbot CBC, and Angela Pulman of Community Enterprise Wales.

This training project identified under-represented women living in a mining community who needed training in intermediate information technology skills and supervisory management skills. The course offered a progression route from a Women in Technology course to a module in Computer Science provided by Further and Higher Education providers in the Community Centre and other routes according to individual need and the needs of the local labour market.

Women who were identified as single parents or with a low income had the opportunity to gain qualifications in management skills with the Institute of Supervisory Management, alongside credits with SWWOCAC and National Vocational Qualifications. Guidance and counselling provided with the DACE Guidance Unit formed an integral part of the course, supported by an equal opportunities policy alongside crèche and transport support. A study skills programme and the use of the library networked to the South Wales Miners' Library were available to the trainees.

The NOW Project
Transnational Partnership

The Women in the Workforce course provided an opportunity to develop further our transnational relationship with VIA and IFOLD.

The project compared and contrasted, within a European perspective, the socio-economic, cultural and political factors affecting women who wanted to enter the workforce. It also studied the impact of industrial change and its effect on women.

Banwen Community Centre with opencast site in the background, post 1993.

Our partners VIA in Belgium provided the necessary link with KEERPUNT (Turning Point), which was an education and orientation (training) centre for women under-represented in Hasselt, Limburg, another former coalmining region. KEERPUNT was established in 1983 and offered long-term unemployed women the opportunity to choose to change career or life direction by giving them assertiveness training, career planning, office skills and guidance and counselling.

We were now developing professional partnerships with women from other European countries, which was an extraordinary development for a small voluntary group based in a small and remote former coalmining community. Subsequent meetings in Brussels, the transnational visits and organising a large seminar all deepened and strengthened our relationship with our partners.

VIA was a 'link' organisation, based at the University in Hasselt in Belgium. It negotiated training for unemployed adults and unlike DOVE was not a provider. Its intermediatory role between unemployed adults and industry was to liaise with managing directors of enterprises and technical schools. It responded to the needs of the local labour market and provided training to unemployed men and women regardless of the status of these jobs. So, for example, if the local labour market demanded that women should do the jobs that previously were done by men, even though these jobs had been downgraded to a lower status, the women were expected to 'fill the gap'. It was KEERPUNT that shared more ideas with DOVE since we both provided

Women in the Workforce: Alternative Choices for Women from Coalmining Areas. October 1993. Teresa Rees, speaking, Mair Francis chair. (Photo by DOVE Workshop)

courses for women from areas most affected by the run down of the mining industry. KEERPUNT and IFOLD shared in a feminist ideology and worked to establish a flexible learning environment that included childcare support, guidance and counselling and assertiveness training.

IFOLD was a non-profit making organisation that delivered training courses to women who were expected to remain at home as carers. During the 1980s Italy's economic development moved at a rapid pace which enabled IFOLD to develop provision for women and to challenge the patriarchal attitudes of the men. We were fortunate to have met other providers on the ERASMUS European programme through our partnership with DACE. Those partners included Bremen University in Germany,

In 1996 Mair Francis was awarded the prize of Welsh Women into Europe in recognition of her work in developing transnational training programmes.

and higher education institutions in Ireland and Florence in Italy. The WEA in West Glamorgan had strong transnational links with its sister organisation in Bremen, Arbeit und Leben. Giulia Scarpa, a part-time tutor and translator from Florence, had visited IFOLD prior to our visit and was able to liaise with us and on further visits became our translator.

We were impressed with the provision for women in both Belgium and Italy, but the difference between DOVE and our partners was that they worked in an urban

> The Belgian and Italian models of guidance and counselling was to be the innovative method most suitable for the south Wales experience.
> IFOLD's and KEERPUNT's objectives of informing trainees of the need to give value to existing skills raised awareness of the legal, social and political implications affecting women's lives and giving priority to women's employment. This is the 'cutting edge' where gender segregation is challenged, where the position of women as low paid employees is questioned. The Sardinian 'Orientamento' guidance model based on equal opportunities encourages women to counterbalance their subordination. This overtly political act is at the centre of their guidance and counselling. Trainees are encouraged not to become more like men in order to succeed in the labour market but to recognise their differences as women and to develop an approach which values sharing, partnerships, co-operation and assertiveness.

environment, making it easier to sustain women-only courses. Our commitment to women-only courses could only run alongside a mixed provision. But what was important was that women in DOVE were the decision and policy makers. We were disappointed that IFOLD was not funding a course in the coalmining region, the Sulcis, in Sardinia. Its funding only supported courses in Cagliari, the capital city, and also co-operatives in the rural areas. In the 1990s Italian women still faced a serious situation as they were perceived as the 'natural' carers within society and expected to forsake their paid work and remain in the home to look after small children or become carers. We were told on our visit that some Italian men believed that the unemployment problems could be solved if women stayed at home. This attitude was prevalent in the Dulais Valley as well. The partnership links helped identify the cultural and political commonalities between women from Wales, Belgium and Italy. So much was shared between the women quite apart from the content of the training programmes: in particular, we shared the problems of juggling work with family responsibilities. Managing the EMPLOYMENT NOW project was in itself a training course for the staff at DOVE and it allowed us to develop our own skills as managers and teachers.

Guidance and Counselling

Guidance and Counselling had become a crucial and significant prerequisite to ensuring that an informed choice was made by potential learners. Mainstream guidance and careers counselling services in Wales were narrow and specific to school leavers and insensitive to the barriers facing women. This provision continued to fail to meet the needs of women, in particular those needing childcare, transport support and a flexible, family friendly environment. Our task was to make women aware of the opportunities and minimise the barriers.

These ideas were brought to the seminar 'Women in the Workforce', mentioned earlier, to be disseminated to other women's training groups in Britain, including women from the Castleford Training Centre in Yorkshire and the Derry Women's Centre from Northern Ireland.

DOVE recognised that it was a relatively easy task to provide education and training courses developed from grass roots organisations and building on social, economic and political experiences. However, sustaining this provision, 'feminising' the training centre and hoping to 'feminise' the workplace was becoming increasingly difficult under a Conservative Government which did not recognise socio-economic and cultural barriers faced by women. There was pressure to adhere to a rigid framework of accreditation, for example, that was anathema to many 'non-traditional' students. Training had to relate to the needs of a market economy, business executives were dictating the curriculum, further education colleges were in effect being privatised and being taken out of the democratic control of the locally elected councils, and childcare provision was seen to be the right of those who could pay and not those in need. To overcome these difficulties DOVE needed to be focused on the explicit social and economic needs of the community. Our agenda prioritised women. It would have been so easy to change the curriculum and respond to the demands of the new Training Enterprise Council's culture, but we refused and became one of the founder members of the Open College Network in Wales. Recognising students' achievement and accessing European funds to provide free courses and free childcare enabled the Workshop to continue to build the confidence of the community.

In this early period DOVE wanted to develop the use of the internet in the way that our European partners had done. On-lining the community was a project that trained women and men in skills to improve the way they studied, to increase their opportunities for employment, to establish a 'telecottaging' business and to encourage parents to support their children's learning at school and at home.

A Community University in Banwen

It had been apparent from 1987 that the Banwen Community Centre was in need of refurbishment. DOVE had been given a grant from the Welsh Development Agency (WDA) to replace the windows and we were in the process of planning an extension to include an extra teaching room, library, children's toilets, disabled toilets, and an extra room for the crèche and disabled access. We were growing beyond the facilities that the Community Centre could offer.

The Access to Higher Education courses and the undergraduate courses which followed later – all provided by Swansea University – now needed more and better learning and teaching facilities. A committee was set up represented by Swansea University, Onllwyn Community Council, Neath Borough Council, British Coal and DOVE to secure new funding. This funding came from the RECHAR Community Initiative of the European Commission, which was adopted by the Commission in 1989 to support the economic conversion of the coalmining areas of the community hardest hit by the decline of their industry and of employment. The Banwen Community Centre was eligible because it fitted the criteria of environmental improvement and restoration and renovation of social and economic infrastructure in mining communities as part of an economic re-development strategy and assistance for training and employ-

ment, and for the retraining of miners and former miners.

Swansea University provided the professional expertise to apply – successfully – for the funding. Building work began in July 1993 and the new extension was opened in August 1994, during the National Eisteddfod Week in Neath, by Hywel Ceri Jones of the European Commission, a keen supporter of DOVE and a native of the neighbouring Swansea Valley.

The Community University of the Valleys

The concept of delivering part-time degrees entirely in valley communities, which became known as the Community University of the Valleys, grew out of the

> During the building renovations classes were dispersed to other community centres, welfare halls, pubs and clubs. The crèche was relocated to the Cwmdulais Community Centre in Seven Sisters and DOVE's office was situated in the staff's homes. Consultations took place with the University and Social Services who gave advice regarding Health and Safety legislation for crèche provision under the Children Act. Nikki Stonelake from the South Wales Miners' Library was consulted regarding the needs for library resources.

vision of DOVE staff, Swansea University tutors and students at Banwen. Dr Sonia Reynolds was employed by DACE at Swansea University to assist in the development of the concept in 1992–93.

According to Dr Hywel Francis the concept of the Community University of the Valleys (CUV) needed to be set against the background of the crisis in the coal industry in the South Wales valleys in the 1980s. In 1999 he wrote in his *Wales: A Learning Country* :

> Crucial elements in that crisis translated themselves into what would universally now, in the 1990s be considered as best practice in lifelong learning but were then regarded with suspicion and scepticism.

He paid tribute to the women-led organisations like the DOVE Workshop which challenged the existing attitudes by successfully providing community-based learning with support services such as crèches, guidance, transport and study skills; the development of partnerships between the voluntary sector and the statutory; the provision of information and communication technology (ICT) and the recognition of innovative European practice through transnational links.

Undoubtedly the CUV provision grew organically out of DACE's commitment to community-based courses in Banwen and it relied heavily on its partnership links with Onllwyn Community Council and DOVE. Like

Teresa Rees and Jane Aaron at 'European Equal Opportunities Day School', June 1994.

DOVE the programme was designed to attract adult students who could not take up educational programmes on the university campus.

The extended Banwen Community Centre provided study rooms, a new conference room, an improved crèche and improved accommodation for ICT teaching. Other funds at the 'start-up' stage had been forthcoming from Neath Borough Council, British Coal, the Coal Industry Social Welfare Organisation

---

The 'On-lining the Community' project provided:

- Accredited training courses in ICT.
- Study skills support within the Access to Higher Education courses and other courses.
- A transnational European partnership with Germany, Belgium and Italy under the EMPLOYMENT NOW Programme. Called Sarn Helen, itcollaborated with European ICT experts who provided the technical and management skills to assist in returning to work.
- The opportunity to establish a telecottaging business in the Banwen Community Centre for the use of former trainees, local SMEs, local authority services such as the Probation Service, Social Services etc.
- Family learning sessions and 'drop-in' internet sessions for primary and secondary schools developed in consultation with the four primary schools and the local comprehensive school.
- Provision for office space and support for SMEs.

(CISWO) and Onllwyn Community Council. DOVE was unable to give any financial help but gave its free time and advice.

At the time the Dulais Valley was targeted by a number of Welsh Office initiatives – most notably the Valley Initiative, launched in 1988 by the then Conservative Secretary of State for Wales, Rt Hon Peter Walker MP – and this meant that the proposal for the CUV fitted into wider strategies for economic regeneration.

The first cohort of students enrolled on 11th October 1993. There were twenty-four students (twelve men and twelve women) who studied Environmental Studies, Modern European Studies and Modern Welsh Studies. Rob Humphreys, the newly appointed Co-ordinator, worked in partnership with DOVE to promote the CUV. Subsequently the CUV grew into a wider partnership involving the Open University and the University of Glamorgan. In support of the CUV partnership a Joint Strategy Group was set up to look at innovative practices to meet the needs of non-traditional learners, and the Open University was able to bring its unique experience in distance learning to the group.

Today the CUV has eighteen strategic partners, thirteen of which are community organisations across the valleys. The partnership now also includes the University of Wales College Newport with its base in Tredegar.

Growing Our Own

During this period the staff at DOVE were all encouraged to attend training courses themselves to upskill. I had

Students of the Community University of the Valleys part-time degree programme, enjoying the sun during a lunchbreak. (Photo by DOVE Workshop)

enrolled on an MSc in Economics and Social Studies and Lesley Smith and Julie Bibby attended a training course in educational guidance. Subsequently Lesley Smith enrolled on the BA Hons part-time degree and Julie Bibby also attended the postgraduate course in Further Education Training Certificate (FETC). Susan Owen, who was responsible for the desktop publishing co-operative, was training at Swansea University to become a tutor for the Advanced Professional Training Unit.

Allyson Lewis, our crèche worker, attended a Play Providers Association course recognised by Social Services as well as doing her English GCSE and IT course.

We were now becoming more interested in communicating through the internet and attended demonstrations on the use of modems organised by Telecottages Wales provided at BP Llandarcy. In April 1993 a modem was installed at DOVE to keep in close contact with European partners.

New Millennium & New Democratic Opportunities

After 1997 with the return of a Labour Government, there were great hopes for new opportunities in valley communities. The arrival of democratic devolution with the founding of the National Assembly for Wales and the securing of European Objective One funding alongside it provided that potential platform for the valleys that had suffered so much. There is no doubt that democratic devolution has provided vastly greater opportunities for DOVE, particularly through Communities First Objective One funding programmes.

The voluntary sector plays a vital role in the regeneration of former mining communities. It sees the importance of strengthening the relationship with local government and the National Assembly so as to stimulate positive activities. In this respect volunteering is central to civic society and DOVE is very much at the heart of it:

Gwenda Thomas, Labour Assembly Member for Neath and Deputy Health Minister and Carers Champion of the Welsh Assembly Government, has written:

The miners' strike served as a catalyst to encourage women to develop their roles within communities, and DOVE has helped women to return to the workforce and also enter public life. Affordable and reliable childcare became a reality in DOVE which took advantage of the Welsh Assembly Government's Communities First Initiative thereby contributing to the regeneration of the Dulais Valley.

DOVE has grown over its twenty-three years of existence and its current specific aims reveal its importance and relevance to social enterprise and the voluntary sector.

DOVE now aims to:

• Conduct research and development projects to evaluate and monitor education and training in the valley.
• Further develop flexible learning for unemployed adults under threat of exclusion and for those seeking self improvement.
• Provide impartial educational advice and guidance.
• Provide essential support structures for those who participate in learning.
• Provide volunteering opportunities for learners.
• Work with the Dulais Valley Partnership and other organisations relevant to the Dulais Valley.

The DOVE Workshop's role has been and continues to be that of an agent for change and DOVE has, as a result of its proactive presence in the community, brought many organisations and agencies together to provide community-based

The Voluntary Sector and Economic Prosperity

Gaynor Richards, Director of Neath Port Talbot Council for Voluntary Service has written:

'It is important to recognise that the sector's contribution cannot be measured in crude economic terms alone.

Voluntary activity generally has a positive impact on the individual involved, and on society as a whole. Voluntary activity takes many forms, and the contribution it makes to social and economic life is extremely difficult to quantify. Providing services for particular groups is often directly relevant to economic activity levels. Work with young children or vulnerable older people, for example, may enable a parent or carer to enter the job market.

Similarly, community organisations that initially appear removed from local economic activity, such as sports and leisure, arts groups, may provide learning and skills enhancement opportunities for individuals who would otherwise remain socially excluded and economically inactive.'

have been based at the Banwen Community Centre to ensure that all members of the community are consulted and play a proactive role in the initiatives taking place. The partnership strategy, initially developed in 1986, was an important development to ensure that existing and new education and training provision would guarantee quality for non-accredited and accredited courses. That local partnership ethos has been and continues to be a constant strategy of DOVE which has been fundamental to its sustainability. The Rt Hon Peter Hain, MP for Neath, then Secretary of State for Wales and Secretary of State for Works and Pensions, stated that:

> From its inception, the DOVE Workshop has thrown a life-line to people desperately needing to change their skills in an environment that required workers to become computer literate to afford them any opportunity of work.
>
> Women had access to a local skill centre which they could fit around their family commitments, and to this day DOVE's position in the Dulais Valley means that people have the same opportunities as anyone else, through a very local amenity. Because of its links with many outside organisations such as Swansea University and its very local input, it remains a contemporary, top class facility, as relevant now as when it was first founded.

education and training facilities. Undoubtedly this initiative has raised the aspirations of adults to learn skills that would help to regenerate the economic, social and cultural base of the community.

The DOVE Workshop has kept faith with the setting up of a community enterprise, the establishing of progression routes from education and training courses to further learning opportunities and employment.

A number of strategy committees

The Local Lifelong Learning Forum

This group was formed in 2002 and had representation from DOVE, the Dulais

Valley Partnership, four local primary schools, two comprehensive schools, Swansea University, Neath Port Talbot College, Crynant Business Centre, Neath Port Talbot County Borough Council's Lifelong Learning Service, and ELWa (Education and Learning Wales – a Welsh Assembly sponsored body that promoted learning for post-sixteens). The forum's mission was to initiate developments of benefit to the community and to ensure that no duplication of provision occurred. This is very much in the progressive tradition of the early days of DOVE.

To date the forum still meets, chaired by Julie Bibby with two new partners, Crynant Community Centre and Seven Sisters Community Centre, the two satellite centres of DOVE. ELWa's representation on the group was lost when that organisation was restructured.

Business Start-up and Innovation

DOVE continues to develop its networking role with a number of organisations, particularly the Dulais Valley Partnership, in order to encourage the setting up of small businesses or co-operatives. Neath Port Talbot Business Connect, Community Enterprise Wales,

Chwarae Teg and the Wales Co-operative Centre gave advice and help to those requesting it. Chwarae Teg together with DOVE organises events to encourage women's business start-up.

Partnership Still the Way Forward

The success of the DOVE Workshop could only have been achieved as a result of partnership with other organisations, not only from the education and training organisations such as Swansea University, the WEA, Neath Port Talbot College, but as importantly from the Neath Port Talbot County Borough Council's departments such as Economic Development Department, Lifelong Learning and Social Services. Other organisations are Business Connect and Neath Port Talbot Council for Voluntary Services. It was very rewarding to know that DOVE was able to address many of the issues identified in Neath Port Talbot's Community Plan 2000–2006 and that much of our work flows from such partnerships and from continued Welsh Assembly and European funding.

Neath Port Talbot Objective One Strategy 2000–2008

The purpose of this strategy was to provide a framework for the delivery of the Objective One Programme in Neath Port Talbot under the Communities Regeneration for Deprived and Peripheral Communities. DOVE received under the Priority 3 Measure 3 European Regional Development Fund (ERDF) Objective One funding of £326,915 towards a total project cost of just over £430,000 to improve the facilities at the Centre. This

> The VIEW (DOVE) Ltd Steering Group today meets bi-monthly. The structure of the Committee represents the community, learners and users; the Co-ordinators of the DOVE Workshop are Julie Bibby and Lesley Smith. The group monitors the financial development of the workshop as well as evaluating its day-to-day activities.

in all our communities. In many ways, we felt, the network was now using the positive example of DOVE's origins and development on a county-wide basis. The project looked at local solutions to local problems and DOVE, Glynneath Training Centre and Amman Valley Enterprise were the inspiration for this approach. The centres provided people with access to information, advice and learning networks to provide for the development of a culture of lifelong learning. The network of centres provided new physical and cultural links between communities, providers and support systems in order to raise skills levels and to improve the employability of people within the County Borough.

Our local authority again broke new ground in another visionary policy initiative relating specifically to the valleys and within which DOVE figures prominently. Its Valleys Strategy encourages every single community to play a more active role in building a vision for their particular valley. The aim of this ten-year plan puts an emphasis on education, transport and social enterprise across all the valley communities.

Derek Vaughan, Leader of Neath Port Talbot County Borough Council, stated recently:

It has been said that DOVE was

improvement helped to upgrade the Centre and crèche and to deliver a café facility which has subsequently operated as a community enterprise available to the wider community of Dyffryn Cellwen and Banwen. Improved disabled access as well as an improved infrastructure has enabled DOVE to expand the number and scope of courses as well as upgrading the facilities provided for existing courses.

The New Learning Network and the New Valleys Strategy

In 2000 Neath Port Talbot successfully applied for European Social Fund Objective One funding under Priority 4 Measure 3 to establish a three-year project to provide access to learning and training through a wide network of Local Action Centres. This was a visionary policy commitment by our local authority to prioritise skills enhancement conceived in strife and born of necessity – it has certainly grown up to be a fine example of what I call active citizenship – people and communities taking a hand in and helping to shape their own futures.

In an ever-changing economic climate DOVE Workshop has remained constant and pro-active in identifying the needs of residents in what was once a thriving mining community. They have striven to develop the facilities and to provide whatever was needed to ensure that students and users of the centre can realise their full potential as individuals and can compete effectively in the labour market. Everyone involved in

DOVE fully embraces the concept of lifelong learning by providing a wide range of services to all generations in the Dulais, Neath and Upper Swansea Valleys.

Neath Port Talbot County Borough Council has made a commitment to bringing forward a stronger, more vibrant and sustainable future for the Valleys of Neath Port Talbot, but this would be impossible without centres like DOVE Workshop.

Broadband in the Community
'Broadband opens new world for ex-mining community'. This was the message from Lesley Smith when DOVE succeeded in receiving broadband. It opened up a world of opportunities for

New signage, linked with the launch of the Community University of the Valleys project, 1993.

Funding for Phase II was approved to consolidate, develop and extend the New Learning Partnership and its work, based on experience gained in Phase I. The project ensured additional progression for new learners engaged at basic level in Phase I. It will utilise additional voluntary and community organisations to access and engage people who are still self-excluded. The funding extended access and delivery of flexible learning, offered additional informal learning opportunities and allowed the additional use of technology such as broadband communication links. Another addition to the project was a scheme that assisted learners with the transition from learning to work or career changes.

local people in and around Banwen with the addition of two IT laboratories added to the teaching rooms, crèche and café. One clear example of the benefits of broadband was the opportunity given to local author George Evans, who was able to research two books on his life as a soldier and miner. This provision also enabled DOVE to open the IT labs for everyone in the community to make the most of the resources.

Lifelong Learning

Providing access to lifelong learning is a key part of the DOVE Workshop's role as a Local Action Centre in the New Learning Network (NLN) – a nationwide initiative supported by the European Social Forum.

In addition to leisure-related and vocational courses, it offers a wide range of qualifications in skills to help people find work and further their careers.

DOVE Today

Dovecote Day Nursery

Initially set up on a part-time basis to support learners attending classes at the centre, the nursery now opens from 7.30 am to 6.30 pm and provides childcare for learners, working parents/guardians and respite care. The nursery is registered with Care Standards Inspectorate of Wales for twenty children 0–5 years of age, and is working to capacity with a waiting list. There are fifty children registered, the majority using the nursery on a part-time basis. The nursery employs six members of staff, all of whom are qualified from Level 2 upwards, and only one staff member, the manager, is project funded, with remaining staff costs covered through the income received. The nursery offers opportunities for volunteering and work experience and placements include those from Neath Port Talbot College, Llangatwg Comprehensive School and Ysgol Gyfun Ystalyfera.

Dulais Valley Under Threes Sure Start Project

The DOVE Workshop employs a Sure Start worker funded through Cymorth. The aim of the project is to support parents with children aged three years and under, to improve their parenting skills and give information and advice on related issues. This is achieved by working in partnership with the local health visitors and a variety of health and education agencies. Two parenting groups are held each year, a Barnardo's Parenting Matters course is held once a year and a number of day schools are held, the topics of which depend on issues raised in the courses. Many of the parents participating in this project go on to enrol in formal education classes and four parents have formed an independent parent support group.

Café Sarn Helen

In January 2004 a new enterprise was formed, a healthy eating café, Café Sarn Helen. The idea for the café came from learner evaluation feedback and consultation with centre users, and coincided with an Objective One project to physically improve the centre. The café is called Sarn Helen because that is the name of the Roman road running alongside the centre, extending from Neath to Caernarfon via Brecon. This identifies DOVE with the Dulais Valley Tourism Strategy. The start-up costs for establishing the café were provided by the WDA Community Tool-Kit and the Coalfields Regeneration Trust, with a tapering grant for three years. The aim of the café is to be self-sustaining and profits will be used to further develop the business.

Sarn Helen Community Garden

The idea for the development of a Community Garden was, in part, a result of DOVE acquiring the lease of Banwen

Official opening of the 'extension on the extension', with Joy Howells, Lesley Smith, Julie Bibby, Hefina Headon and Mair Francis, January 2004. (Photo by DOVE Workshop)

Community Centre, which meant we could access funding to re-develop the centre, and take the opportunity to improve the land surrounding that had, until that time, served no purpose. At the same time we were was struggling to find fresh produce locally for our newly established healthy eating café. We were also receiving feedback from the community that they were experiencing the same problems. We attended a number of events that highlighted the concern about poor levels of health in our communities. As a result of all these factors the community garden developed an idea that has been met with enthusiasm by local residents, funding bodies, and other partners that we work

with other communities.

The 'Grow Your Community' project has three distinct phases. Phase One created a learning garden in the land surrounding the DOVE workshop. This garden is used for horticulture classes, environmental awareness raising, linking with local schools and colleges and growing small amounts of produce to supply the on-site café.

Phase Two is reviving disused allotments and in the long term will create a market garden owned by the community to supply fresh inexpensive produce to its residents. In 2007 the funding body, Big Lottery's People and Places, awarded the DOVE Workshop a three year grant to

DOVE is proud that the curriculum offered at the centre is planned by the centre staff in negotiation with providers and community development workers and takes into account those identified needs and current strategies and statistics. In addition to the formal curriculum offered, DOVE offers informal learning opportunities through the use of day schools, work experience and volunteering. Current course brochures are available at the DOVE Workshop and its satellites; course information is also available on the website www.doveworkshop.org

further develop the project.

Phase Three will be a partnership project to build workshops to house the Dulais Valley Partnership's Countryside Warden Scheme and serve as a shop front and workshop for the allotment revival.

New Learning Initiatives

Situations sometimes arise when identified learning needs cannot be meet by the providers. In those cases DOVE will seek funding to develop and accredit (if appropriate) the relevant course. The following are two examples. Firstly there is a local history course entitled 'Fact, Fiction or Both?' This was designed in response to the Dulais Valley Partnership's tourism initiative, in which a number of sculptures and way markers have been strategically placed in the Dulais Valley at sites of historical interest. The aim of the course was to raise awareness of the initiative and encourage the course participants to be 'ambassadors' in their community, to appreciate their surroundings and raise the profile of the valley.

Secondly as a result of working with the Dulais Valley Partnership's Youth Worker a need was identified to offer young people aged fourteen and over the opportunity to learn work preparation skills such as interview techniques, job search and job applications. DOVE developed a unit of learning that has been accredited by the Open College Network Wales.

Basic Skills and Educational Guidance

In April 2006 DOVE employed a Basic Skills/Guidance Worker to provide support and information for the users of the centre. The role of the worker is to assess the skills of the learners and offer the appropriate support, whether working one to one or negotiating with education providers to offer Return Classes. The worker also offers individuals signposting information and formal educational guidance and the opportunity to visit courses to encourage learners to progress. This is a crucial post for DOVE as it offers the opportunity to gain feedback from learners which will be used to inform future curriculum and support services. It gives the learners the opportunity to voice any concerns in a confidential setting and to discuss their learning needs with an experienced worker.

Strengthening Working in Partnership

DOVE has been fortunate to develop key partnerships since the late 1980s. One new partner is the Welsh College of Horticulture. Today these key partners include the following.

The Dulais Valley Partnership, which is a Development Trust, was set

Mair Francis, Dr Hywel Francis, Lesley Smith and Rob Humphreys with Lord and Lady Callaghan in 1995.

up to address socio-economic issues within the Dulais Valley. DOVE has a director's seat on the board and is represented on the Finance and Policy Forum and Lifelong Learning Forum. Its co-ordinator, Stuart Douglas of Seven Sisters, is a valued ally.

The Cwmdulais Uchaf Communities First Partnership was established in 2002; DOVE is represented on this partnership and has been involved in the consultation process and the development of the Action Plan for the Upper Dulais Valley. The Cwmdulais Uchaf team are based in the DOVE Workshop and work closely with DOVE. The co-ordinator, local activist and graduate Dean Cawsey, is a DOVE 'enthusiast'.

DOVE is a partner on the New Learning Network project, an education and training partnership that supports

Local Action Centres and satellites in communities across the County Borough of Neath Port Talbot. DOVE is the Local Action Centre for the Dulais Valley and has satellite provision in two centres throughout the valley.

The Community University of the Valleys Partnership (CUV) is a unique partnership between the higher education and voluntary sectors in West Wales and the Valleys region, working to develop appropriate community-based higher education opportunities. DOVE has been an active partner, proudly since its inception in Banwen in 1993, when the first CUV Part Time Degree Scheme to be held in the valleys was provided in the Workshop.

Alongside this DOVE is a partner of the Community Progression Partnership, the aim of which is to widen access to higher learning by making provision more accessible to those who would normally be excluded from gaining a higher level qualification.

Valuing Volunteering

The courses and the projects take into account national and local strategies. DOVE's work with the Dulais Valley Partnership addresses the issues identified in its Strategy for Regeneration. This is an example of how the voluntary and community sector makes a significant contribution to the local economy by directing its activities at the most vulnerable groups and deprived communities in society, making it an important stakeholder in the Welsh Assembly Government's efforts to counter social exclusion. According to Gaynor Richards, Director of Neath Port Talbot CVS, there are currently an estimated 1,110 voluntary organisations in the Neath Port Talbot County Borough and a further 1,217 organisations based outside the borough, but providing services in the borough. There are 1,485 employees, of whom 947 are full time. Each year, 61,583 adults volunteer in Neath Port Talbot. The voluntary sector in Neath Port Talbot contributes £100 million to the economy annually.

Flying into the Future with DOVE

The DOVE Workshop Development Plan 2006-2009 brings the development of DOVE up to date. The current key issues addressed by DOVE are:

- An ageing population base.
- A high proportion of elderly and retired people.
- A high level of long-term illness.
- An above average rate of unemployment.
- Low numbers of formally educated people.
- Changing employment demographics.

The DOVE Workshop now has two satellite centres at Crynant Community Centre and Seven Sisters Community Centre. A small number of 'starter' courses are delivered in the satellites and the learners are encouraged to progress to higher level courses based at DOVE or other appropriate venues. The satellite centres are owned and managed independently of DOVE; however, working in partnership with those organisations ensures that 'first step' education provision can be offered literally on the doorstep.

The DOVE Workshop has continued with the same democratic management structure established in September 1984, with the Steering Group, made up of users and community representatives, and representatives from Onllwyn Community Council and Neath Port Talbot County Borough Council, meeting bimonthly. A key local representative and long-time supporter from the very outset has been Councillor (Ali) Alun Thomas, now deputy leader of NPTCBC.

Since 1989 the DOVE Workshop has successfully developed what was previously known as a community enterprise but is now known as a social enterprise, which allows the organisation to further develop the childcare facilities and have the opportunity to seek new ways of financially supporting their charitable aims.

The DOVE Workshop will continue to work in partnership with vital partner organisations such as Neath Port Talbot County Borough Council's Economic Development Unit and their European Office and Lifelong Learning Service, the Employment Service, Neath Port Talbot College, the WEA and Swansea University, and new ones such as the Welsh Assembly Government's Economic and Education Departments and Careers Wales West.

DOVE addresses a number of issues identified within the themes of Neath Port Talbot's Community Plan 2002–2012. For example, within the Education and Training theme DOVE is actively promoting 'the importance of effective continuity and progression within the context of lifelong learning' and offers 'access to impartial information, advice and guidance to overcome the barriers of learning'; the Economic Prosperity theme states the importance of 'increasing the availability and accessibility of affordable, high-quality daycare' and 'encouraging entrepreneurship at all age levels'. DOVE also promotes entrepreneurship, has established a social enterprise that has created nine jobs, provides a day nursery for working parents and supports other community development organisations in the Dulais Valley.

The 'Better Health and Well-Being' theme states that we need to: 'promote healthier lifestyles through developing effective initiatives to, for example, improve access to healthy foods and exercise'. In 2003 DOVE opened a healthy eating café to challenge poor diet and promote a better lifestyle. DOVE is working with the Health Promotion Unit to offer healthy eating demonstrations and basic cookery courses for young mums and dads and the Sarn Helen Community Garden will promote a 'green gym' mentality and provide access to healthy food.

DOVE addresses at least three of the National Assembly of Wales' A Winning Wales identified priorities, Making Wales a Learning Country, Promoting Information and Communication Technologies, and Creating Strong Communities. This is done, as ever, holistically by removing barriers to learning through the provision of a day nursery; good physical access; being community based; and offering individual support to learners; by providing lifelong learning opportunities ranging from informal learning to level 5 accredited learning; by offering opportunities for work based learning through our projects; by providing access for all members of the community to ICT facilities with up to date software and good connectivity; by supporting the Dulais Valley Partner-ship, a development trust and the Cwmdulais Uchaf Communities First Partnership; and 'by encouraging people from all backgrounds to gain confidence and the skills to participate in their local communities.

The Welsh Assembly Government's National Basic Skills Strategy for Wales (2001) recognises that: 'one of our key aims is to reduce, as far as possible, the literacy and numeracy problems among adults'.

And in that spirit, DOVE has now created a full-time post for a Basic Skills Support Worker to ensure that learners are assessed and given support to improve their skills.

Looking to the future, DOVE has some exciting and visionary plans. They include:

• Carrying out consultation work in the Dulais Valley to inform the development and implementation of the Dulais Valley Learning Community Plan. The work will involve focus group sessions with targeted groups such as young men, lone parents, the economically inactive etc.
• Writing a Learning Community Plan in partnership with the Cwmdulais Uchaf Communities First Partnership.
• Planning future curricula in relation to the findings of the Learning Community Plan, taking into account the County Community Plan and national strategies and priorities.
• Continuing to support and develop the Sarn Helen Community Garden project.
• Training a member of staff as a Front Line Guidance Worker and Basic Skills Support Worker.
• Continuing to support the work of the Dulais Valley Partnership and Cwmdulais

View of Banwen, post opencast mining, with ponds and tennis court, 1995.

Uchaf Communities First Partnership and ensure that all projects work in synergy with other initiatives being implemented in the Dulais Valley.

• Continuing to carry out staff appraisals and encourage staff development to meet the future needs of the organisation.

Remembering Our Community Roots and Looking to the Future

Lord Callaghan, the former Labour Prime Minister and at the time President of Swansea University, was a keen supporter of DOVE and the Community University of the Valleys. He wrote this personal message on the occasion of the opening of the extension in 1994 and it is fitting this history ends with his inspiring words:

I have never forgotten my first visit to Onllwyn nearly fifty years ago. The occasion was to speak at a meeting shortly after the election of the 1945 Labour Government.

We were full of plans for the future and when the meeting ended, we went on discussing what we would do for so long that I missed the last bus back to Cardiff.

Since those early days, Banwen has seen many ups and downs, but despite all the difficulties, the community has never given up and I am delighted that through the efforts of so many different authorities, the newly extended Banwen Community Centre will continue to be a lively focus for the life of the community and will be of prime importance in the continuous process of education and training that we shall need in the future.

Good wishes to Banwen, and the best of good fortune to a stout-hearted community.

Bibliography

BOOKS AND JOURNAL ARTICLES

Aaron, Jane, Teresa Rees, Sandra Betts and Moira Vincentelli (eds), *Our Sisters' Land* (Cardiff, 1994).

Campbell, Bea, *Wigan Pier Revisited: Poetry and Politics in the 80s* (London, 1984).

Cope, Phil, *Chasing the Dragon: Creative Community Responses to the Crisis in the South Wales Coalfield* (Ebbw Vale, 1996).

Elliot, Jane, Hywel Francis, Rob Humphreys and David Instance (eds), *Communities and Their Universities: The Challenge of Lifelong Learning* (London, 1996).

Francis, Hywel, *Wales: A Learning Country* (Swansea, 1999).

Francis, Hywel, and Mair Francis, 'Social exclusion, active citizenship and adult learning: building new learning communities in old coalmining areas', in *Adult Education and Democratic Citizenship*, vol. 11 (Krakow, 1998).

Neath, Dulais and Swansea Valleys Miners Support Group, *The Valleys Star* (1985–86).

Rees, Teresa, 'Feminising the mainstream: women and the European Union's training policies. Women, Wales and Europe', in *Equal Opportunities International*, vol. 12, nos 3–5 (1994).

PAMPHLETS AND REPORTS

Dulais Valley Partnership, *Strategy for Regeneration* (1996).

Francis, Mair, *Report on NOW Project Visit to Cagliari, Sardegna, Italy* (1993).

Neath Port Talbot CBC, *Objective One Strategy, 2002–2008.*

Neath Port Talbot CBC, *Positive Futures: Towards a Valleys Strategy* (Consultation Document, 2005).

Neath Port Talbot CBC, *Western Valleys Strategy: Positive Futures* (2006).

VIAE, *Next Step for the Valleys: Regenerating Valley Communities through Adult Education* (Ebbw Vale, 1990).

Winckler, Victoria, *Ambitions for the Future* (Bevan Foundation Research Paper on the Valleys, Tredegar 2003).

The DOVE Team

The photo on the cover of this book features some of the leading ladies of the DOVE team.

Back row from left to right: Julie Bibby, Susan Owen, Lesley Smith, Mandy Orford, Glynis Howell, Jill Douglas, Susan Carter, Gillian Watts. Front Row from left to right: Moira Lewis, Mair Francis, Joy Howells, Hefina Headon.

Julie Bibby

I was born and brought up in Dyffryn Cellwen, the daughter of a miner who was on strike during the Miners' Strike of 1984, at which time I lived in Aberdeen. I returned to the valley in 1986 with my three children and became involved in the DOVE workshop by attending a Mother & Toddler group. I continued my involvement by attending courses, and gained employment through training I became an ICT tutor, and in 2000 became one of the joint co-ordinators at DOVE. I feel privileged and proud to work within my community in an organisation that is so highly regarded.

Susan Owen

I married my husband in 1983. He worked at Blaenant Colliery in Crynant between 1970–1990, and I supported him throughout the 1984–85 miners' strike. My daughter Jessica was conceived and born during the strike. When my husband was made redundant, I enrolled on a computer course at DOVE Workshop to up-skill and further my employment prospects after bringing up my children. With the support of Mair and the staff at DOVE I was encouraged to train as an IT tutor. I'm still at DOVE; I'm now a Community Garden Project Worker.

Lesley Smith

I was born in Crynant, my grandfather and father were colliers. I left the village with my parents in 1967, however I returned to the Dulais valley in 1985 with my own family. I first visited DOVE Workshop in 1989 to join a 'taster' programme, I remember walking into the building and feeling welcomed and encouraged to put aside my anxieties about returning to study. My personal journey, with the support and encouragement of Mair and Julie, has been a definitive one, however I hope it is a journey that others have also experienced who have benefited from their involvement in the organisation.

Mandy Orford

I've lived all my life in the Swansea Valley. In 1984 I got married and was working at Lucas (old Tick Tock). After I had my two boys, in 1992 I enrolled on an IT course at DOVE. I later got a job in the South Wales Miners' Library which had a branch in the DOVE Workshop; to support DACE (Department of Adult Continuing Education) courses being offered at the centre. I still work at the South Wales Miners' Library and I'm proud that our branch library at DOVE is still open and well used.

Glynis Howell

I was a striking miner's wife during the 1984–85 strike, and also a mother of a newborn baby. At that time I could see there would be changes ahead in the working environment. The courses offered at the DOVE Workshop provided me with the new skills needed to get back into the job market, as well as being an opportunity to meet people living in the Dulais Valley – being an Ystradgynlais girl originally! I have worked for the Local Authority since 1992, but that doesn't mean I've stopped learning. I'm now studying for a part-time degree in Humanities. This wouldn't have been possible without the support of the staff at DOVE Workshop. I have also served as Chair of the DOVE Steering Group for the last eight years.

Jill Douglas

I was born and bred in Seven Sisters with a father and two brothers who worked in Blaenant Colliery. In 1981 I moved to Germany to work for a British Forces family as their nanny, 1983 saw me marrying a serviceman and in 1993 we returned to Seven Sisters to live. In September that year I was employed by Mair Francis to work in the nursery at Dove. In the fourteen years I have been with Dove I have seen the establishment go from strength to strength, and being part of the organisation and what it stands for is an honour.

Gillian Watts

I was born in Pantyffordd and I am a daughter of a mining family. I supported the set-up of DOVE Workshop and remember numerous meetings and travelling around in the mini bus to gain the support of the community. When DOVE was established I attended a number of courses including the first European funded women-only course to be held in the centre that taught women video production skills. I went on to a full-time catering course in Neath College, whilst still retaining my links with DOVE. In 2003 I returned to the organisation as the manager of Café Sarn Helen.

Susan Carter

I was brought up in Onllwyn, both my father and grandfather were colliers. When my daughter started school I attended an IT course at the DOVE Workshop. Soon after I started working for Swansea University's Department of Adult Continuing Education providing secretarial support on their Community Part-time Degree. I was based at DOVE Workshop for eleven years and enjoyed every minute of it. I now live in Ystalyfera and work for Neath Port Talbot County Borough Council, and still maintain my links with DOVE.

Moira Lewis

I was born in the Dulais valley, a daughter of a miner and represented the Onllwyn Community on Neath Borough Council from 1976 to 1996, becoming Deputy Mayor in 1988 and Mayor in 1989. From 1984 I was a member of Onllwyn Community Council until 1996. I also served as a Magistrate for nineteen years. I was a supporter of the 1984–85 miners' strike and became the Founder Chairperson of DOVE Workshop. It has been a great privilege to have been involved in an outstanding initiative of which I am extremely proud.

Mair Francis

I came to live in the Dulais Valley in 1976 and worked as a supply teacher from 1977. I am a granddaughter of a miner and a tin-plate worker and I was a supporter of the miners in the 1984–5 Miners Strike. In 1986 I became the Manager of the DOVE Workshop which gave me and others the opportunity to develop ideas established during that year. In 1999 I left DOVE and in 2003 I become President of the DOVE Workshop. I am very proud and honoured to be part of such an exciting initiative in the valley.

Joy Howells

During the 1980s I was a member of the Dulais Valley Peace Movement and visited the Peace Camp at Greenham Common where I became friendly with Mair Francis. Later I attended marches and meetings during the miners' strike

and was subsequently invited to join a group of women who were contemplating a new project. I attended my first meeting of DOVE in 1986 and was very impressed although I could not possibly imagine the outcome of such a venture. With Mair at the helm in the early days DOVE became well and truly established. I have attended meetings and courses throughout the last twenty years and still feel impressed by the commitment of all who have enabled this excellent establishment to continue.

Hefina Headon

I am the daughter and wife of a miner. During the miners' strike of 1984 I was secretary of the Neath, Dulais and Swansea Valley Miners' Support Group, active on the picket line and I spoke at many political meetings alongside trade union leaders, politicians, actors, singers and musicians. I organised fund raising events, travelled to other coalfields and many parts of Britain alongside my involvement in the distribution of food parcels for the miners' families. I was a founder member of the DOVE Workshop and also attended courses and represented DOVE at national conferences.